MEMORIES OF CHILDHOOD:
LIFE IN THE ROMANIAN ORPHANAGES

By

Nicolae Viorel Burcea

§

Originally Published January, 2017, Berlin
3rd Edition, June 2021

Table of Contents

–

A Brief Introduction, Part i
A Personal Message

I remember as a child being told by my adoptive mother and others that I had a special story to tell to the world. It was mentioned to me that what had happened to me was remarkable given the circumstances: that I was a boy placed in the horrid Romanian orphanages, that I grew up there without developing detrimental physical issues, that I managed to read and write somehow, and that I was adopted (such a rare dream for orphans) by American parents. I was blessed and watched by some divine being, I was reminded. I was a miracle, and it was my duty to announce to the world that even though bad things occurred, I somehow escaped and survived them all. Something like that.

In the orphanages, I felt very special, for reasons that I am not sure why, and in America, I seemingly doubled in my belief that I was even more special, given my circumstances. This invincibility probably derives from the story of my life: something difficult and awful happens, I somehow escape and survive it nearly intact, and the cycle repeats over and over again, each time getting more and more daring as I grow older. It is easy to believe that something "hovers" above, making sure that just enough happens, but not enough to completely destroy me. At the end of the incident, all that remains is a great story to share with others. And the greatest story, I supposed, was probably my time spent in Romania.

Of course, some context is important here. My story, it's true, is very special, especially given my circumstances. I was not a baby when I was adopted; I was actually much older. I am Romani by blood, and though many orphans are Romani, the fact that a Romani boy was selected for adoption is bewildering to many Europeans (when others would have chosen white children). I did not have many medical issues when I came to the United States, but being fully functional in the orphanages had traumatic effects on my mental health when I left, since I not only was exposed to everything, but I understood things that were happening and came to develop certain beliefs about the world from them. Finally, I was adopted in 2002, a year after international adoptions in Romania were outlawed. The adoption was legal, but the battle to push three separate courts in Romania to finally overrule the lower courts and allow the adoption to go ahead is a miracle in itself. It cost my adoptive family untold tens of thousands of dollars and hundreds of paperwork, questions, and tests. All for one boy.

When I was 12 years old, I thought that I was so special that I should start recording my life story as soon as possible. I began writing, but I stopped after several chapters because I was not sure if I really knew what happened in the orphanages. For some reason, as a child, I had conceptualized the orphanages more from an emotional perspective than a narrative perspective. I wrote about the crying and physical pain, and I couldn't provide a linear perspective of these things. So, I was confused and opted for poetry, which better suited me at that time. I tried many times since to write the story of my life, but I was stumped over and over again for the same reason: how do I connect pain in a single straight narrative? It seemed impossible. I took many notes and kept these notes for many years. I started the book well over a dozen times, each time trying a different format. But I never completed any of these tries.

One day, when I was 21, I met a Kurdish refugee in St. Louis who asked me to write a book about his life. He couldn't write his story, he said, because he didn't know how to. So he asked me to listen to his oral story and write it as I saw fit. So, I spent three days listening to him. I took many notes and found that he was doing the same thing I was doing; sharing the pain but not his life story. Pain is clearly easier to vocalize, especially because it's so personal, but it's not easy to write from a historical perspective. But this man helped me see how I could sort through it all and conceptualize it more accurately, from a third perspective. Namely, I could combine the idea of pain by touching on growth, and add a cohesive narrative to it as it proceeds to the end. So, what that means is simple. Every time you experience pain, something happens to you. That difference is growth. You grow in some way, whether you realize something new about yourself and others, you change your behavior, or you have emotional understanding- you grow. Pain is a fuel of some sort to make someone act differently. Often times, people recall pain in very direct moments, and these moments serve as "links" to a narrative. Nobody remembers their whole life, step by step, but they remember "links" of their life that defined them very strongly. In common terms, these links are called "memories" and they serve as important tools for our understanding of ourselves.

So, after listening to my Kurdish friend, I went home and wrote down all my memories of the Romanian orphanages. And suddenly, I could rearrange them from a historical, biographical, perspective. I sat down and started writing them, one by one, and within a month, I finished my book. It's amazing how something like this happens, but it does. I wrote my first book so quickly, and with such fluidity, that I don't even remember exactly what I did as I was writing them. It seemed natural.

One thing to note about these memoirs is that they are very blunt and direct. That is the result of note taking. I had a lot of notes from my early drafts from the age of 12 upwards to age 17. Most of these drafts are authentic, meaning that the recollections were as vivid and accurate as they could possibly be. They were written from a very young, simplistic, and unexperienced mind. I retained that vocabulary in these chapters as they are pretty exact to how I thought back in the day. I tried to refrain from using current understanding of my past from what I had thought about my time in Romania when I was a child. I think it is important that I wrote the book from the notes I took when my memories were fresh and vivid to me.

Therefore, the book isn't edited from a narrative point of view. Some sentences were corrected grammatically, and many expletive words were taken out (unless I felt they otherwise would hinder the meaning of the sentences). I tried to retain the chapters in their original parts, and I think I have made clear to readers what was written later in my life and what was written when I was a child. My sentences become longer, vocabulary improves, and rules of grammar are followed through. Hopefully doing this hasn't interfered with the story very much.

My final comment about this book is its mission. The book was originally written to do one thing: record the facts of what my time in the orphanage was like. I felt it was important to just know what happened so that I could better understand how I became the person I came to be. However, as a young boy of 12, I had another thing in mind. I wanted to write a book that served as a historical document about Romanian orphans. There isn't much information about what Romanian orphanages were like in Romania or across the globe, especially from the perspective of a Romanian orphan, and I felt that it was my duty first and foremost to fill that page in history that was blank because I actually knew how to read and write. Therefore, the book's aim is to be a historical document, a historical autobiography. I cannot claim to know what other orphans did in Romania. I was actually surprised one time when I met a young Romanian orphan who went to a mentally handicap orphanage; I didn't even know these buildings existed, so it goes to show that there are many things I don't know that other orphans experience. My story should be a personal chapter in the long line of Romanian orphanages, which is scarce and almost nonexistent. I hope that this chapter isn't erased, and will serve to show that kids like us existed. It's a dark chapter in Romania, and I have encountered many Romanians who don't and can't believe what happened to us orphans. The world tends to view Romanians with great negativity about this subject, and I actually did not want to add to that idea by producing "another" Romanian horror story. I understand how Romanians will be defensive about this. I also understand that many Romanian orphans are too focused on survival to care about who has pity on them. The best way ahead, for me anyway, is just to ensure that what happened becomes a public conscious fact. It existed, period. It was horrible, period. It's a part of Romanian history, period.

As I grew older, I encountered some Romanian orphans who utilize their past histories to their advantage, whether publicly or personally. They have become puppets to their past, constantly victimized by themselves and others, airing on sensationalized shows on Romanian television and otherwise. This is utterly pathetic and despicable to me. It was one of the reasons why I did not want to publicly publish my book; I had a fear that I would showcase this idea of being a victim and desire everyone else to feel sorry for me and my life. This is outrageous. I don't want people's pity and I don't desire people to victimize me for what happened. Part of my ability to do so well in my life is because I grew up in a Romanian orphanage where I learned to be independent and make the most of myself. Using other people's sympathy for me is an undignified and low way of benefiting yourself. So, I want to make very clear that this book should, in no way, be used for this purpose. This book is not something for people to feel sorry for orphans. It's not for you to feel sorry for me. It's not something to use to condemn Romanians. It's a historical document about what happened to one orphan. One, of course, whom you have to understand, had an extremely lucky life. He was adopted. That is important to know, because it changes everything. Most orphans who write books on orphanages are adopted, and so they tend to have a different perspective of what orphanhood means than actual remaining orphans. Some of those adoptive kids have utilized their past life in deplorable ways for their personal benefit, and it's simply not right to all other orphans who continue to suffer to be exploited like that. This book does not aim to exploit orphans and orphanhood. It's a story of one boy in this condition for several years. That's it.

A Brief Introduction, Part II
A History of Romanian Orphanages

As this book aims to give an autobiographical historical account, a background foundation of Romanian orphanage history is important to know. Romania, as far as I know, have had orphans for a long time. In this particular chapter of history, however, the Romanian orphan crisis has a singular event. It is the result of Decree 770 in October 1966, enacted by Romanian dictator Nicolae Ceausescu. The purpose of this act was simple: to industrialize faster, Romania needed more workers, and to get more workers, families had to have more kids, and to have more kids, abortion was outlawed and women had to have more frequent sex. To have more children was heavily incentivized, both politically, economically, and socially. For this reason, unsurprisingly, there was a huge boom in the number of kids a family had.

The Romanian economy was not sufficient at that time or any other to sustain individual families with such a growing population, and for this reason, many families decided to allocate their children to local government institutions to raise them instead. That occurred for some time, and these institutions became massive, housing well over a million children at one point. That meant that anywhere between 1 in 20 Romanians were raised in an orphanage at some point in their lives.

There were a variety of reasons why Romanians placed their children in orphanages, and many Romanians agree that money is probably the biggest factor. A great deal of orphans, surely 50% or more, are *tigani,* or Romani, such as myself. I've heard and read stories about Romani families placing their children in orphanages and getting them out when the kids were much older and able to work. I've also heard that children were placed in the orphanages because they weren't planned or wanted, or that a family conflict occurred and the child leaving was the deciding factor. Whatever the case, very few orphans actually knew why they were in orphanages. Many of them, such as myself, hardly knew anything but orphanages, having grown up in them nearly all our lives. It was rare to receive visitations from family, and when it happened, it was always the idea that the child was going to be taken out soon.

The orphanages were, as the world has come to find out, inadequate places to raise children. Many of them were old buildings, being previously wards or hospitals, schools, or warehouses. Very few were designed to be orphanages. The conditions inside were often horrible, being always very cold, very old, and often dangerous. Given the fact that chaos reigned in these orphanages, the places were destroyed and run-down even further. A reoccurring aspect of these orphanages was their smell; dried urine and the smell of dust and age.

Many of the people hired to be caretakers of these institutions were some of the most uneducated and corrupt people imaginable. These people, it is important to note, do not represent the Romanian people as a whole. Romanians in general adore their children and try to always give the best and most of what life offers to them, cherishing them over everything. The Romanian people, I have noticed, put their families above almost everything save money, which often goes to their families anyhow. Family is everything. So it may seem strange that these orphanages contradict this very Romanian cultural trait. I am not sure how to explain this.

These caretakers were often very simple-minded and easily triggered. Some were extremely vicious, and every orphan surely has a story of one or two special caretakers who was specifically cruel to them somehow. The caretakers had, if I am to be honest, one of the worst- and hardest- jobs in Romania. There is simply no way that 20 or so women (for they were mostly women, from my experience) could control 200 or so chaotic children without being violent. This is an unrealistic expectation on the women, just as it is unrealistic for a mother to be perfect in raising her child. We orphans were psychologically disturbed, scared, and aggressive. We fought each other constantly for everything: food, clothes, candy, and care. To control us, our caretakers utilized their most effective actions, which almost always included violence, to keep us in line. The horror stories that people hear is what happens when caretakers lose their humanity and suppress children to incapability of action or any form of independence. The worst thing a child could be was to invoke personal independence.

As time went on, the orphanages swelled, and so did street children, kids who escaped or got kicked out of these places as they aged out. There was no actual plan for what to do with these kids. It may seem reasonable to assume that kids in the Communist times were probably sent to work in big factories or farms to become low-income laborers. However, after the 1989 Revolution, the institutions fell and everything became quite chaotic for all Romanians. I am sure that Romanian orphanages took a different turn then.

I have never met a Romanian orphan from the communist time (1966 to 1989) after the decree was made effective. I am sure that many exist, but I have never met one. I am sure that orphanages operated differently at that time as well, probably having more structure than what I encountered, given that they were seen as numbers to exploit rather than being forgotten and sidelined after the Revolution. Children born and raised in orphanages from 1966 to 1989 are referred as "Ceausescu's Children", given that they born and raised under his regime. I am not sure what kids after the Revolution are referred to but they certainly got more attention. International media had seemingly flooded back in Romania in the 1990s and exposed the horrible conditions of the country and its orphanages. It's a dark chapter that many Romanians well remember and want to forget very vigorously. For a country that values their family and western ideals of freedom and human rights, the orphanages were a complete national humiliation. The fact that there were so many orphans, all of whom were related somehow to the national population outside those chaotic walls, meant that, as a people, Romania had simply allowed this occur and turn a blind eye to it. It is understandable that many Romanians felt speechless by the horror and simply couldn't comprehend it themselves. Many who sidelined the issue by stating that they were poor and incapable of taking care of the children were drowned out by international fury and horror. After all, the world responded, these caretakers *are* Romanians. The people did this to their *own* children.

Something this complex is hard to explain to world. And it has tarnished the Romanian conscience, feeling the whole weight of this guilt. Not only were they poor, had the bloodiest communist revolution, was in dire need of assistance as Europeans, but they also committed atrocities to themselves on their own soil. For many Romanians, orphans were the last things to feel sorry for. After all, everyone suffered. Everyone was anxious and worried for their lives. Everyone did the best they could with what they got, which wasn't much. The entire country was an orphanage, one Romanian once told me.

Since the airing of international media exposing Romanian orphanages, Romania acted swiftly to undermine the conditions or even blame the world for exaggerating the conditions themselves. Because the media exposed so much of what had happened, the Romanian people were horrified and couldn't believe what they were seeing. The government shut down international adoptions in 2001 after it came to light that illegal adoptions were occurring, some to slavery in different parts of the world. An aggressive campaign was made to get rid of orphanages and do away with institutions. Massive campaigns were organized to fight for the improvement of disabled and orphaned children. They continue to fight for these rights today. Is the issue gone? Hardly. Someway, somehow, many of these orphans have somehow disappeared. I don't know what happened to them or what became of them. Orphanages have been shut down, destroyed, torn down, and new buildings have been built on top of them. Files and papers have been destroyed or gone missing. Names have changed and whole memories have disappeared. Not only has Romania been swift in seemingly getting rid of the problem, but also making it disappear. I was really horrified when I went back to Romania and found my orphanage had gone away and become something else entirely. My biological mother was horrified when I told her a little of what happened inside them. Even she didn't know. Most Romanians don't know.

I don't know how to appease orphans. They're kids, anyhow. Many are too hurt and angry to receive letters and verbal statements of apologies. Many of them have died, given that they were already malnourished and physically sick in some way or another. They have been traumatized by horrible conditions and seemed forever scarred by what they lived through. I have never met one that lasted through it all and came out to have a good and decent life, though I suspect some do exist. Should this ever happen, this would be a miracle to me, for Romanian children are often so scarred that any hope of a good life seems almost near impossible. What to do, in consideration of what had happened, is not a question I can answer. I feel that the best I can do is just to make sure that this memory does not go unchecked. Why is it important to make sure people remember? They say it's because we must ensure it never happens again. I say it's because no matter how bad your past is, it's still who you are and what you've done, no matter how ugly it is. The ugliest part of our lives is often the most truthful aspects of who we are as humans. They make us who we are just as our strengths make us the things we wish to be.

Number of State Children and Orphans in Thousands*

Number of Children in State Care and Orphanages between 1990 to 2010

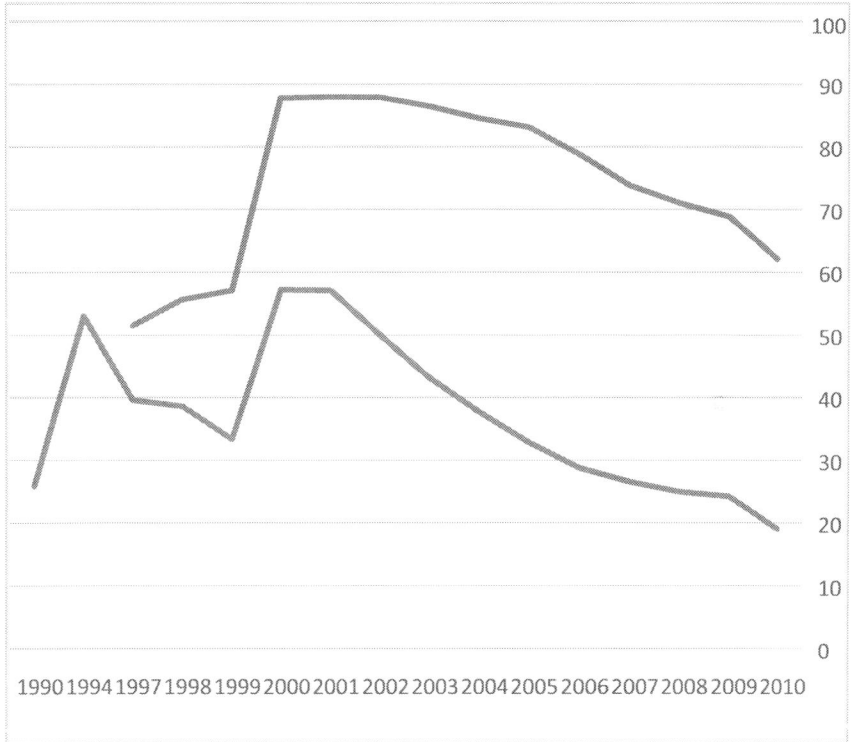

Orange line: number of children living in orphanages
Blue line: number of orphans in state care

*Info derived from the National Authority for Child Protection and Adoption, as well as statistics from the Ministry of Labor, Family, and Social Protection of Romania.

MEMORIES OF CHILDHOOD:
LIFE IN THE ROMANIAN ORPHANAGES

-

PART THE FIRST

Whereas I was Born and Recall My First Memories

I was born on December 6th, 1993 in Bucharest, Romania. This day is a very special day, for it is St. Nicholas's day and, I presume, the very reason why I was given my name. My mother, I was told and I have read, was very young when she had me, about 16 or 17 years of age. It appears that there was some dispute with my mother and my father, and my mother's parents, and all this led to some chaos in which I know little of. The result is lost in memories I hardly know of, and, for this reason, much of it remains very absent from my knowledge. Everyone says very different things, so that perhaps I shall never know what really happened the first several years of my life.

The origin of my beginnings in the Romanian orphanages are disputed, as well, for there are two versions of how I got into the homes for children. The first, to which I took to be true by my adoptive mother, was that I was placed in the orphanage when I was about four and a half years of age. I really don't take this to be wrong, mainly because I remember being in orphanages for a relatively long time, for at least three or more years. The second story, told to me from my biological mother, was that she had simply dropped me off at the Mănăstirea Cașin (Cașin Monastery) when I was seven years old. I remember a great deal about the Cașin Church, but I had no idea it was a monastery, and I do not recall me spending much time inside the church. Also, I remember three distinct Christmases in Romania, which means that I had to be much younger than seven years when I went into the monastery. I don't really know whose story is true, for much of my childhood has been a mixture of truth and myth, and as such, I often opt for what's logical and what I can remember. As such, then, I take my adoptive mother's account to be most accurate, although in truth, there is a lot I still haven't found out about my early life.

Another reason why I tend to agree with my adoptive mother is that I remember ages seven and eight extremely well. In fact, a majority of this book focuses on these two years, whereas ages six and five I remember less and less. I would have clearly remembered being dropped off at age seven, because I remember so much when I was that age. Unfortunately, I remember very little of the church, and I remember much before seven, and all those memories was when I was in orphanages. So, I will start from my first memory, which, taking my adoptive mother's account, was when I was four years old.

My very first recollection I have is when I was very young, and I was outside on a children's see-saw. I was alone on the see-saw, and I had a thick sweater on. The see-saw I was on was a very long one. There was a bench on either side, where a number of children could sit and bounce from, for the see-saw bounced up and down; it did not necessarily go directly up and down as one would think.

This moment is my first memory, and while this was not important, the distinction in this memory was that I was looking up and I saw that a man was looking at me very distinctively. I remember this startling me, and making me feel frightened, and I was scared, but I do not know why. The wind was cold, or maybe I was cold, but, either way, everything was cold and every time I think of this memory, it makes me shiver. I do not remember this man at all, what he looked like or what he had on, I just recall this feeling he instilled in me, of complete terror and fear, and this memory sticks with me for all time.

I move on, then, to the orphanage in the city. If I am correct, this orphanage was extremely close to the one that I would inhabit when I was about seven or eight years of age. In fact, there were two orphanages I would inhabit in that same area, but to which the exact names I have forgotten. If I am not incorrect, and my logic has not gone mad, this first orphanage, which was close to the other two I would later inhabit, was very close to the Cașin Monastery. Although I do not recall going into that church as a young boy, it is possible that I might have gone there, or that this monastery had a close association with the orphanages around it. Needless to say, it doesn't particularly matter. My first orphanage was very close to the Cașin Monastery, and the Arcul de Triumf of Bucharest.

I remember this orphanage for the trees it had about it, and the cribs that we lived in a large part of our times. I don't remember how long I was there for, or how I came to know how to speak, but by the time I left, I knew how to speak well, and to run and play. I remember that I was quite good at climbing anything, whether it was my crib or the trees. I remember hearing a great deal of noises, such as children crying and cars honking. I recall humming to myself a great deal of time while I was in the orphanage, but I do not recall any personal abuse. But, then again, I remember bits and pieces and not much else. These memories are like horizons of sleep for me. I can recall them as good as I can recall dreams, which is quite poorly.

There is, however, one thing that I do know. I know that after I left this orphanage and went to the next, I knew what the right thing to do was and what the wrong thing to do was. I am not sure how I knew this. After all, I recall myself being a troublemaker since I barely can remember anything, so it seems that I had a good sense of observation and thought process. Although many people tend to disagree about my level of understanding at such a young age, I feel it is important. I want people to understand that I lived in the orphanages subject to observation and thought processing. I learned quickly and I observed a lot. For some reason, I was able to distinguish from the many things that was occurring, and I was able to take that in consideration every time I did anything.

My next destination I remember relatively well, though not in chronological order. I don't remember how we got there, but I remember that when I we did get there, the orphanage was very large and had a very big gate. I know that the backyard was surrounded by a big high wall, and that there was a big tree in the middle of it. Here, technically, is where my story begins, for it was there that I got to know what being an orphan was like.

PART THE SECOND

Whereas I Recall the Second Orphanage

The second orphanage will always stick in my mind as the one orphanage that matches up exactly to the ones portrayed on news media. The building was falling all over the places. Everything seemed lost and forgotten. Windows were broken and cribs were everywhere. The smell of urine was especially strong. Outside, the air smelled of mud and earth wherever one went. I remember the area being especially rainy most of the times.

When we were taken out of the buses, we were all taken to the big main room. Here, we were taken to our rooms, which were three big white rooms, one open doorway leading into all of them. Each room was filled with cribs side by side. The mattresses were really old and clearly falling apart. Luckily for me and my crew, we went to the very back room, and these cribs and mattresses were white and seemingly new. Even the room was new, and it had huge windows that saw everything outside. But we had no pillows or blankets. It was just cribs lined up against other cribs. When sleeping, it was hard to tell whose crib was whose because our cribs were so tightly stacked together.

Each room was divided by age, and the back room was for us younger ones. We got new caretakers, and I remember one very clearly, for she would become infamous in the orphanages for her cruelty and mean demeanor. It was at this orphanage that I recalled my very first memory of getting hit and made fun of. However, I was too young to be much of anything, so I was very passive most of the time. I often stood in silence and did not say much. I usually stuck to myself and sang songs. I did often lie a lot and argue, but most of the time I acted like a typical orphan. I just went about my days finding occupation in various activities that filled my day. This orphanage was quite weird compared to the later ones because it was really boring. Nothing happened. We usually were huddled in the main room, being watched and overlooked by the caretakers.

I do recall that I became really quite more thoughtful and curious at this age. I'm not sure what gives me this impression, but this was a thing about me that was happening. I recall getting yelled at a lot for being too "nosy" over things. I would adventure out in the night and stray away from the group and look at different things when we went on extrusions.

There were only three big things I remember at this orphanage particular orphanage: there was the big Hollow's Eve day, the great celebration, and the night scenario that somehow sticks with me forevermore but doesn't seem to be a reason why.

As a unit, the orphanage was really quite terrible. Every day, there was crying. Kids got beat up for everything, no matter how small the act was. There caretakers seemed to have little to no patience for anything. The walls had a lot of holes in them because a lot of kids would punch them. The aggression level was really quite scary, and I must admit that I started to show signs of aggression as well. I would get into some fights and even would say no to the caretakers, although I would take it back the moment I got hit.

Almost everyone stold. This was a fact of life for me, and I guess, everyone. My food was stolen almost every day. I would often eat as fast as I could the moment the food was poured or given to me. I would have it finished by the time I got to my table because I knew that the other kids would take it from me once I got there. The food was terrible, however, and, thinking about it now, much of it did seem as if it was expired. However, I was always hungry, so I ate whatever I could. The only good food in the orphanages was not the food but the hot sweet milk, the one in the pot. It was like soup to me. I would trade my food for other people's cups of hot milk because the milk tasted good and filled me up faster than the food did.

The other kids often acted like staff, and this was a real issue in the orphanage because of the chaos that ensued. I naturally came to realize chaos and orphanage were almost inseparable, but, at the time, this was new to me because before that, I was usually in a crib. Honestly, other kids deciding what I should do made me scared and angry most of the time because I was really young and almost incapable of defending myself. If I was sexually abused, which I don't really recall (but the probability is definitely very high), this orphanage was probably the one place where it must have happened because, at the time, I was not very aggressive.

Another thing that was relevant in the orphanage that I remember is the fact that some kids were often treated quite terribly by the caretakers. Some kids, you know, they had some kind of mental issues. So, they would be tied to something so that they didn't leave the place that the caretakers wanted to be. They would sit there and suck their thumbs. In fact, I did that all the time, but a lady had put hot sauce on my thumb and my mouth nearly burned. Not only did I stop sucking my thumb that instant, but I developed such hatred for hot sauce that I won't even try salt and pepper today because it has a strong flavor.

It really became so commonplace for us kids to get hit and abused that I came to think this was very natural. In fact, if you, the reader, think that I seem to have a very matter-of-fact way of retelling the abuse and horrible situations, it is partly because I learned that these kinds of things are normal. Unlike other survivors, like a Holocaust survivor, the happenings of the orphanages were seen as normal because there was nothing else to show us what things could be like; there was no better "before". The world that was is the world I thought was now; for this reason, I never viewed myself as a victim. I would go around and see a kid get hit so hard his back would bleed, but this did not phase me. I learned to tune the crying and screaming out. I learned to not care that someone was going to get beaten. I tried to avoid getting beaten as much as possible. This desire to avoid connection or being seen is the main reason I ended up being viewed as cold and indifferent. I learned very young that everything was unfair. However, it isn't just unfair to me, it is unfair for everyone. That is the law of life. This is what I learned and accepted as a kid.

I'm going to pass the details of unfairness and talk about the big celebration our orphanage had. It was hosted by some charity people, which is extremely common in the orphanages. Charity was often how we got parties and new toys. Otherwise, we had practically nothing.

In this specific moment, another very important aspect of the orphanage life was discovered and observed. Whenever outside people came to the orphanages, the caretakers and the boss would try to tidy things up. There was usually a cleaning and we all got better clothes to wear. Maybe a shower or two, but there was too many of us. So, the shower consisted of us going outside naked and being sprayed down. We could have just stood in the pouring rain and the caretakers would have called it a day. Of course, the pump was really powerful, so this whole scenario was quite comical. Everyone would push to go to the back to avoid being hit by the water, for it hurt. Especially because the water was always cold.

So, the caretakers would become different. They would treat us nicer and the boss would act like she cared about us, when it was clear she didn't. A lot of toys would be in her office, but we would never see them, though she would always promise that she would give them to us if we acted good. But it never happened. In charity events, we were told to smile and be happy. Naturally, that wasn't too hard to do because anyone who was not a caretaker seemed to act nice to us and we responded by being happy anyway.

I will admit that we all became really selfish the moment the charity people would hand anything out. On that particular day that the charity people came, there was an older woman who was giving us handmade sown handkerchiefs and chocolate candy bars. The way we swarmed up to her and literally took the candy out of her hand is quite appalling, but, at least for me, I felt I had to do it because all the candy would disappear before I got to her. Indeed, kids were grabbing at least two or three and then running away. There was so much fear in getting things- it was as if we felt that her goods would disappear before our very eyes. Indeed, patience and waiting your turn, and the rules of being fair, were almost nonexistent in the orphanages. Needless to say, we carried on that day, playing a number of games while the charity people from the village or town came to make us food and play music. It was quite fun actually. We were certainly the center of attention and it was clear that the caretakers all bit their tongues and wouldn't rebuke us in front of these new people.

It rained that day. I remember it clear as day. It rained and all the caretakers and charity people ran for cover under the big tree and tents, but we orphans stayed out in the rain, continuing to play. I think this made the charity people feel very strange, for it was literally pouring. But, out of nowhere, the rain became lighter and a huge and clear rainbow appeared in the sky as the sun came brightly behind the clouds. It was the first time I saw a rainbow and everyone suddenly thought it was a sign of God or something. Meanwhile, while everyone was staring up at the sky, we orphans had found the watermelons and were cracking and eating them, which seemed to really piss off the caretakers, but the charity people seemed really to take pity on us, and offered us more food. I think everyone was stuffing themselves with food because it was unusual to have so much food everywhere.

Later that day, or maybe the next day, new people came in and gave us solar glasses, where you could put on these glasses and stare directly at the sun. Through the glasses, the sun would appear like the moon, where you could see its outline. I'm not sure what or why we were doing this, but we received a lot of charity events in the orphanages that seem to bring with them a lot of things that had no relevance to our lives. Indeed, to us, they were like entertainment and a distraction from the beatings. Of course, I don't want to demean charities, for they mean well, but I am relating how I felt when I encountered them.

That day, I remember stealing someone's solar glasses because I think I broke mine. The guy who I took it from got really mad, and I remember running for my bed when he saw me with his glasses. Although he never did beat me up, stealing his glasses made me feel excited, like I had won or something. It was a thrilling experience that I would continue long after I left the orphanage. The next big moment in that orphanage was the Hollow's Eve night. The caretakers had dressed as ghosts that night, and I was literally freaked and scared for many days afterwards. The reason why this was a big deal for me was mainly, I think, because of our location. Our orphanage was in the countryside. We were surrounded by a big brick wall. Every now and then, we would peak over, but all that anyone could see was forest upon forest. This observation was really scary because I didn't know what lay in the forest or beyond it. I was used to the caretakers telling us scary stories, but I did not really take them to be stories. I was pretty naïve about everything, so I took the stories to be fact. Thus, I really believed in fairies and ghosts and werewolves and big demons who kidnapped you, and all these things. The one story I particularly remember was one about a beautiful girl. Apparently, if I ever went into the forest alone, I would encounter her and want to kiss her. But, when she came close enough to me, she would kill me. I know now that this is a

Romanian folklore, but then I took it as fact. What's interesting about that Hollow's Eve night is the fact that even though I didn't trust anyone, I believed anything anyone told me. Many orphans were like this. Indeed, I grew up to be very superstitious about a lot of things.

The final thing that's to be said about this orphanage is a moment I had one night. So, one night, as I was in my bed, wide awake as was typical of me (it was natural for me to fall asleep in late at night, like 2 or 3 a.m.), I saw the full moon come out, and the light flooded our whole room. Everyone was bathed in this eerie moonlight, and I felt incredibly uncomfortable. I recall how silent this scenario was, and the silence- yes, the silence- was really scary. I was so accustomed to loud noises and constant movement that when things seemed peaceful and silent, it felt awkward and lonely. I was really afraid of this feeling-loneliness. It's hard to describe this feeling. Silence is loneliness at probably the most acute level. There is just no explaining it. It's a terrible feeling and state of being.

Anyhow, I was in that orphanage for several months and not much longer. A group of people came and soon we were told to pack what little we had (what did we have?). We were escorted outside of the main gate, and big buses came. We were one by one called to get in a group. It was devised by age and height (I don't think many of us, including myself, knew how old we were). Once rounded up, we were told to get on a bus. Then, the buses left down the dusty road. I recall that we were on the last bus, and that I had a chance to stare out the window and look at the orphanage. It really looked as if it was about to crumble. It looked so empty and ghostly that I quickly looked away. Its mere existence seemed to disappear now that we were leaving. It was as if it was becoming part of the forest, unknown and forgotten.

However, I did glance back just enough to see that one caretaker was closing the big front gate. The sound of that gate closing will forever be on my mind. Because, right when I heard the gates closing, I thought about the screams and crying that I heard almost daily. And the gate closing-suddenly, all the sounds in my head went silent. It was as if something had died and didn't exist anymore. Looking back at the orphanage, I didn't even seem to notice it. I just saw the weeds and bushes surrounding the walls. Everything seemed ghostly.

I sat back in my seat and looked about me. Many orphans whose faces I didn't know too well seemed to squirm in their seats like me. I was going somewhere new, and this seemed to make me nervous. All my friends seemed to have disappeared. Everything was starting over and it felt really tragic. But, with an attitude I would come to maintain throughout my time in the orphanages, I laid back and started singing a song. There wasn't anything I could do anyway. No sooner had I contemplated the thought of not caring about what was going to happen when the bus jerked and off we started riding. Outside, I stood up and saw the rolling hills that are so common of Romania stretch out endlessly. As I put my face to the window, I could feel the vibrations of the bus as it moved on the road. I think I must have sung a whole symphony by the end of that trip, the musician that I was.

PART THE THIRD

Whereas I Become Troublesome and Have an Interesting Encounter

We drove in the city of Bucharest late in the evening of that day. I remember specifically seeing the Arch of Triumph getting bigger and bigger as we drove up to it and thinking that Bucharest was a magical place to be in. I had my mind set on being perfectly happy for the rest of my days. However, that would prove otherwise, as I was going to find out later that night. The bus dropped us off by a large orphanage and quickly left. Everyone was placed in a large group inside to be assigned where to go. This was the common way of doing things. Usually, kids were placed in different rooms by age or the preference of the caretakers. For the rest of the time in the orphanage, kids hung out with their groups they were assigned to on the first day. For me, on the first day, I was assigned to the room in the far back, with all the deformed, crippled, and handicapped kids. This was mainly due to my skin color; I looked different.

I was a tigano (gypsy). This wasn't something I was really aware of at the time (that I was a minority), but I certainly could feel its presence. I wasn't aware, at the time of the stereotypes people had about tigani because everyone around me acted Romanian; a majority of Romanian orphans were tigani like me, so I didn't think much of it. I knew that tigani were musicians, and this was often related to me because I was prone to singing all the time, but I never understood this concept. As such, I don't really associate with that culture and identity because I knew nothing of tigani people or even their language and customs. I considered myself a Romanian like all the other orphans. I do recall wondering every now and then why my skin was not white, like the other orphans (and the typical Romanian), but I never gave it much thought. I was aware that people didn't like us and would often call us scums, but in the orphanages, this was almost irrelevant because so many of us were all alike. I wasn't overwhelmed by the stereotypes of the tigani people, and I hadn't any clue that what those differences meant for me. Although I experienced racism all the time, I never understood this. I, in fact, would never come to understand this because I had no way of understanding how these stereotypes related to me. Of course, I stold, lied, cheated, and tried to manipulate people to get things. I did not perceive this as a tigani thing; this was clearly because I was often hit, lied, and cheated to. These actions only happened as a result of my environment. However, I did feel very comfortable doing them because I learned and mastered them well, and when there was a chance to be nice to people, I never knew how to be nice or to be fair. It is weird to say now, but as a child, I did not know how to be a good kid with good manners. I did not learn how to be like this, so when I did do something good, I was clumsy at it. I would share food, and give something to someone, but then quickly pull it back, take a bite, and give it to the person. When they took too long to take it, then I just assumed they didn't want it. I never suspected that their hesitant behavior was actually a sign of politeness.

Well, in the city, they do not like tigani. I would learn this soon enough. In the previous orphanage, nobody cared. I'm not sure why. We had different caretakers now, so that might be why. Or it may be that country people may not care that much. Or I may be wrong. It's most likely that I hadn't been exposed to a lot of outside adults in the past, so they had no chance to really rebuke me. Thus, I may have learned that I was just as equal as the other boys. But in the city, this was changed dramatically.

Anyway, I was placed in the back room with mostly handicapped kids or people that were like me. This orphanage was the first time I met my first friend. His name was Ionut, which is pronounced like Yonutiz, and that's the best way I can pronounce it in English. It's a very Romanian name, but he was a tigani boy like me, and a little bit older. He was a very practical person. Not logical, but rather practical. He and I were often unalike, but somehow we got off to a good start. I believe that he offered me a piece of cigarette candy and I've liked him ever since. He was very loyal and thoughtful of people, although it's hard to ever think orphan boys being generous and that way. I will say that he treated me that way, but not everyone else. We became like brothers.

The orphanage was situated very much in the middle of a big street. Thus, it became the "Orphanage in the Middle of the Street" as everyone called it. By it was a huge playground, a big pool that we never used or worked, and a whole line of junk yards behind it. We spent a lot of times in doors, mainly in the center of the big hallway on mats listening to the boring stories that the caretakers said and watching a little TV that was always fuzzy. If you want to know what we watched, that I do not remember. It must not have been very important. But we listened to a lot of music, most particularly the newest pop music that came out which, I can tell you, was pretty good at the time. We got different kinds of people that came over and treated us. Yes, one nurse came every few days or so to check on us. Do not be fooled, though. She was rather awful. She would either refuse to treat us tigani or give us really crappy care. Always us handicapped people were treated like shit. I don't think I really minded though, because the care she gave the other orphans wasn't very good either. There was a time when I was incredibly hungry and I sneaked into the nurse's office and stole the medicine. Then I ate it all. It was those little pills that are made of wax and have different colors. They look like mike 'n ekes. They tasted so bad that I just ripped them open, poured out the powder, then I ate the outsides. Anyhow, most of the medicine the nurse had in her little office tasted really bad but I did try them all.

My attitude here in this orphanage took a relative twist. I say this for two reasons. Firstly, in the past, I just stood back and observed everything. However, I soon developed this idea that I had everything figured out. That my biggest weapon was telling lies and blaming others for what I did. It hit me hard the first time I realized I could manipulate people. I found out I could get what I wanted not only by avoiding pain but also by actually getting my immediate desires met very quickly. It all depended on how you said things. Orphans would go ask the caretakers for something and they would get a knock in the head. Another would do the same thing, sometimes in a sorrowful way, and get what they wanted. I realized that talking good was a whole lot more effective than being mean. So I went around telling lies that others have said and improving upon them in different circumstances. In time I became quite good at it, until I became notorious for it. In fact, one of my ideas was to tell many people individually a different story in such a way that they would all be confused about what really happened. I realized a lack of communication amongst everyone made for less beatings. Now, while this sounds really cunning, I must add to the point that it was practically impossible not to lie in the orphanages. The beatings from the caretakers were rather bad and would scare me and everyone else quite a bit. Lying was, in essence, one of the only ways I could avoid being beaten. Even though it's taught that lying is a terrible and awful thing to do, many of us orphans would beg to disagree. I couldn't count the number of times lying was an effective tool for me, both to get my way and to avoid getting beaten. It was just practical. You had to lie, for it was a really cruel world. This is the first and most important law of life.

So, like the previous orphanage enhanced several times more, I became troublesome until my very name was recognized as pretty bad. Caretakers would often call me the "little devil" and all kinds of names that implied evil and everything that went along with it. For I became highly defiant. I would refuse to obey anybody, which was an unheard of idea that occurred very rarely and came along with heavy beatings. That was another thing, too. I would get beaten very badly. Amazingly, I would heal quickly (almost by the end of the week), and the beatings would just make me worse. I became more aggressive, which meant I squirmed around a lot and even would run around so that the fat caretakers would not be able to catch me. In this way, I was glad I was small and thin because I was much harder to catch and keep up with. I would run out of the orphanage until the caretakers couldn't chase me anymore. Then, when they got really tired, I went back inside, where I would have to repeat the routine a couple of times before they finally gave up and were fed up in trying to beat me. I would come in all proud and arrogant and say a lot of ridiculous things to the caretakers until they got mad again. Then, late at night, while I was sleeping, they would take me by surprise and tie my legs together, then proceeded to beat me while I tried in vain to untie myself and avoid all the beatings at the same time. It's quite hard. It was my own doing, though, and I knew it.

As for the abuse, well, it was quite bad. I say this in a very serious tone. And it was not exclusively the caretakers anymore. It would be the older kids. They would try to form groups of their own. I assume they realized very early that they could protect themselves better if they ganged up. Most of the rooms had an acknowledged leader. The room kids would be the gang and one kid stood alone in being the one everyone looked to. Those influential kids had rather similar personalities. One of them was being able to cuss extraordinarily well. However, most of the traits that stood out was definitely the ability to get along with everyone easily, being bossy and confident about it, and being highly athletic. Being physically fit has always been a trait admired by orphanage-type facilities. Some of the kids became influential by the caretakers having a liking to them, thus the other kids knew they could rely on them to soften up to the caretakers to get what they wanted. However, these influential kids, which there was a lot of, always competed with the others, so there was a lot of fights and kids trying to downplay the others and trying to get them in trouble.

Almost every one of them tried to enhance his "position" by giving themselves noble titles like "king" or "duke", whichever sounded the nicest at the time, and would definitely overplay this fantasy world by proclaiming their right hand favorites as "princes", or next in line as "crown princes", or their favorite girlfriends as "queens" and their other favorite girls as "princesses". Any boy in their group that showed any sign of physical fitness would be declared as a "guard", which were then assigned to whomever needed them (or otherwise, whomever actually wanted them), and the ones that showed exceptional expectations were then made "knights" or "gangsters". The girls were not so idealized, but they were treated like special property to those deserving of them (which happened to be all the kids that thought they ran the place). Girls were always seen as irrelevant in orphanages. None of the boys liked them, and most girls hated us. The caretakers always treated the girls better than us. They were seen most of the time as very passive, and so therefore very weak. And there is nothing an orphan boy hates in others than showing weakness. You don't get hit or slapped and don't respond back. The more indifferent you are to beatings, the more you could fight back harder, and the more perseverance you had, the more respect you got from everyone, from the caretakers down to the other orphans.

So this was the routine. One might ask how this all turned out. Actually, it went pretty well. Everyone was in some kind of acknowledgement about this social order, and even the caretakers didn't seem much affected by this, although they would mock this whole idea and even snicker remarks about it as they beat kids up. But this fantasy world was play for everyone. It was weird, because nobody seemed to get tired of it. All the influential kids created a code on how to declare "war" with one another, and things of this sort. They would line up outside in the big playground with sticks that acted like swords and handmade bow and arrows. Everyone in the orphanages had wild imaginations.

Playing in these wars was very fun; especially the stick fights and the bows and arrows, which were not badly done. Some orphans had figured out how to make them very well. If I remember right, one went out in the woods and found the most perfect piece of flexible branch of wood. Then, preferably a rose bush, we would pull up the tough yet flexible stems and bite the stem until we peeled a rope like bow string off of them. The string would be good as long as it was wet and slimy, otherwise it had to be replaced. But it was strong, and the string was skillfully tied to the other branch we had, and then the whole thing was watered, and quickly dried. Afterwards, we placed the bows by a moist place by the orphanage where the pump was and then we went out to look for arrows to make. The best arrows happened to be the ones that were often times the hardest to reach because they were way up high in the trees. But when we managed to get the sticks, then everything pretty much was fun afterwards. I would speculate that the farthest I've ever seen a good arrow fly was about half a football pitch. The bows and arrows were well crafted and prized by whomever made them, including myself. It was against the rules to take someone's bow (and it was considered bad luck, especially if that person had been beaten in a conflict) but it was free game to take the arrows when a "battle" began. The "battle" was quite simple.

Everyone would line up the Spartan way, with the strongest in the front, face the other opposing team on the other side (who was quite a little bit away), and in either of three ways fought. For stupid disputes, a person on each side would fight the other and whomever won would get what that group wanted, sort of like a dual. The other way was pretty stupid as well. In a well-ordered way, if the dispute was "noble" then the group would march up against the other and fight. The last way was just an all-out fight. Consider these battles in comparison to American football. Everyone is just trying to win. And if you think we wouldn't like being hit around or having aimless arrows flying at you in no particular fashion to distract you (and hopefully hitting you in the eye), then you probably see no point to football, where a strong defense tackles you probably just as brutal as an all-out fight.

Finally, the fantasy world was enhanced by a million other little quirks those influential kids would make up. One kid had it that anything that was silky was his, because to him only royal people had silk. Another had it where four people would carry him on a board when he was going "somewhere special", which was in no particular place that I recall. The girls would continuously make fake crowns from flowers or decorated pots. The "kings" would hold "ceremonies" and talk endlessly about stupid stuff that mattered little to anyone. Nobody really cared. So, why did everyone go along with it? That's a good question. I supposed everyone felt important and part of something, as if they were special and unique as a "knight" or "King's Messenger". People ironically feel the need to connect with others, so this may be the way it is done in a deprived world. Or it may just be that the kids wanted to play, and acting out their fantasies was quite the same to them as little kids who put on football gear and pretend they're all-star pro NFL players. It makes them happy, so I assume it made the orphans happy pretending they were back in the medieval days, where everyone was noble and mighty.

I was often excluded from this social game because of my status as being handicapped and in the "back room". Remember, our group was a whole different scenario. My big room was filled with kids that were retarded or handicapped some way. There was only me and Ionut as the most sensible of them all, and nobody liked us, so we were like the outcasts. This is not to say that we were always put down and were always lonely. I caused a lot of commotion in the building. We both were troublemakers, and we pretty much went around trying to mock all the "kings" and caretakers. Ionut introduced me to sneaking out at night and looking through the garbage for food, which was like paradise finding all the stuff people would throw away. I don't especially remember at the time what we did many of the nights we snuck out. I know Ionut was pretty familiar with city streets and he showed me around and probably directed me every step of the way when I was out.

However, in the orphanage, one thing I did like to do and did often was have duels with people. I have always had a fascination with Roman gladiators, and so I would always pretend to be one. In fact, this fantasy of mine was taken to very dangerous levels. I would start fights just to feel like I was in a ring fighting tough duels. Naturally, everyone would gather around when these fights occurred, and this was the usual entertainment. Respect was won based on how well a person had fought and if he won. It was around this time when I started developing a very arrogant attitude about myself, and even started to believe that I was somehow royal and superior to everyone because of who I was. I have no idea where these conceptions came from, but they certainly carried over in my later years in life.

Other than that, I have two last memories of this place. The first one occurred, ironically, when I was taking a crap. We had no toilets in the orphanage, so everyone pretty much pooped in a bowl, which the caretakers rarely cleaned (in which we had to clean daily). There was a big room where everyone crapped in, and it was kind of a comical social gathering. Well, anyway, an old caretaker came inside the room where we were taking a crap, and flatly told me that my mother came to see me. The whole room went dead silent, for this never happens in an orphanage. I became skeptical. I honestly thought it was a joke. But the caretaker told me to hurry up. So I did. She escorted me to the door where a couple was standing outside. It was an older looking lady (I mean like 40s or early 50s) and a man, whom I presume could have been about 30. I saw absolutely no resemblance whatsoever in the couple to me, for they were too old and where not dark-skinned as I was. But nothing was said, and they just walked in and sat down. The woman had a plastic bag of candy and she let me have it. I don't remember what we talked about because I was eating all the candy (which there was a lot of) and not paying attention to the questions she asked me. I know she asked how I was and who my friends were. Things like that. I answered briefly and remembered to stuff some of the candy in my pocket for Ionut. The man did not speak a word. It was a kind of unusual meeting. It lasted only briefly, as long as I took to eat the candy, and then they left. I'm almost confident they were not my parents. After all, it would definitely go against my documentation, where they said my mother had been in her middle teens when she had me. But that occasion really made me wonder. Did those people know my mother? Could she not come, so she had some of her friends come and bring me candy and find out how I was doing to tell her? I'm not sure if my speculations are true, but they did make me feel eager to want to see my mother very badly.

Secondly, there was one good moment in the orphanage I remember quite well. It was the big party, just the day before we left for the next orphanage. A charity came. A really big one. In the early morning, they came to the big playground and hung cookies by strings unto anything that stood: trees, merry go rounds, swings, monkey bars, pavilions, everything. That coming day, they brought in clowns on sticks that gave out cookies to all the orphans. All of us forgot just about everything and ran around trying to have fun. The main people had tons of games for us to do, mostly competitive ones, whereas the winners would get awarded ribbons and prizes. A McDonald's impersonator was there doing magic tricks, which completely fascinated us beyond belief. The charity people brought in bands and musicians, which was really cool because we could ask them to play the latest song at will and they kindly (and patiently) would. We played a lot of football and drank loads of juice. We bobbed for apples and kept them to eat when we were done. They served loads of fruit and cookies. I was nearly stuffed with food so that I purposely threw up so that I could continue eating. I felt I was never going to eat this good of food ever again. Overall, the day went amazingly fast and wonderful. It was the second time I felt I was truly a kid. As the sun dropped, they all said goodbye and left. But all of us stayed outside while the night sky was coming in, watching in silence the hundreds of balloons that was scattered in decoration everywhere on hung trees. One of the caretakers, who was drunk, took her cigarette lighter out and lighted a couple of the balloons, whom instantly popped and made a loud noise. We all cheered. However, the lady told us to shut up. I'm not sure she was supposed to say it, but, while drunk, she told us to shut up because we were all leaving the next day for "relocation". Then everyone said nothing more. I bet everyone was probably thinking where they were going, and all the friends they would lose, and probably that their games and lives they had just got used to was now going to change yet again. So we sat outside in silence, deep in thought as I tried to wrap everything around my head. Then it got cold outside, so we all went inside. Everyone headed for their rooms to go to sleep. Whereas usually going to bed is a chaotic event with a lot of noise and complaining, this time everyone just went to bed in complete dead silence. Tomorrow, everyone was going to have to say goodbye. The halls would become empty and the rooms silent. The sunlight would come through the broken windows and reveal the dust that lay on the floors and beds. But the dust would rest this time, because we were all leaving.

PART THE FOURTH

Whereas the Next Orphanage Stay Was Brief and Eventful

The next day, us kids were rounded up and split in groups on whomever could fit on the buses. Most kids tried to stick together so that they could go to the same orphanage. However, that became almost impossible with so many kids, so many of us were split according to age and how big we were and definitely how many seats were available in the buses as they came and went. No one was immune to separation. Ionut and I were split up. We took it as a matter of fact. He went with all the kids his age. Somehow, I was stuck in the back so I ended up being placed on the last bus, which happened to have older kids and teenagers, all of whom didn't look too happy to see me, or anyone else for that matter. Few of us knew each other.

The bus drove us far into the country, quite a long way from Bucharest. There, we were dropped off at an orphanage that was completely surrounded by a brick wall on all four sides. The orphanage itself was small, probably able to contain about 80 orphans at most. Inside, our bedrooms were nicer than the ones in the previous orphanages. The beds were more plentiful and higher. There were actually bed sheets on them, though still no pillows or bed covers. I don't remember much of what this orphanage was like because we spent the majority of the time outside.

Yes, and the punishment was reduced tremendously. The caretakers were older and not so cruel. They let us play outside as much as we wanted. They talked amongst themselves a lot, smoking almost nonstop, and drinking so much beer that they were drunk the majority of the time, unable to distinguish us orphans from the regular caretakers. It was easy to manipulate them, but the consequences afterwards were pretty bad, as they found out after they were sober and ended up beating us until they wore out. So, we left them alone and did what we could not to piss them off.

I remember it being cold, so it must have been fall or winter. Outside, the caretakers would sit in those cheap plastic chairs and make fun of us when they got bored. One of them had a laser that she would shine against the brick walls. We were so ignorant of the red dot that we were like dogs and cats, hopelessly trying to catch the little spot and wondering almost in amazement where it would go and however it could be so fast. It would never occur to us that the caretaker controlled the little red light, that she could turn it off and on and move it according to her will. Remember we were all ignorant, having absolutely no education whatsoever. What inferences we made happened to be wrong and stupid. For example, I originally thought that the sun was Jesus, because the religious priests said he was the "Light of the World", which I took to mean literally. I thought that the reason why people couldn't stare at the sun was because Jesus was so awesome that you couldn't really look at Him if you tried. Now at night, I thought that the moon was Lucifer, because the religious priests said in the Bible he is referred to as the "Morning Star" or "Light Bringer", so I thought he was only second to God but not as bright and awesome as Him. I had no realization that the sun was a star in space (I didn't know there was an outer space. In fact, at the time, I thought the whole world was Romania), or that the moon was just a blob of rock floating in space reflecting light from the sun to earth. I was a pretty stupid kid back in the day, but it certainly made me awe the natural everyday world.

There was a most unique object behind the surrounding walls in the back of the orphanage. It was a red fire truck, old and unusable, with the long steel stairs fully lifted up. Now, I have no clue how that ever became like that or why anyone would leave a fire truck with its stairs way out, reaching high for who knows what. It gave us a lot of fun trying to figure out how to get to the stairs though. We finally figured out that if we piled kids upon kids, we could individually climb onto the wall and basically jump onto the fire truck and climb the stairs. A lot of kids, including myself, fell from the stairs because the wind was really strong many times and we all lost our balances. We landed below into the bushes. I can tell you the falls were very painful, for we got plenty of scratches. One kid got so bruised up that one of his eyes got scratched and he went blind. Luckily for me, I only fell twice, and from then on I always stayed very close to the middle and hung on for my life, moving very slowly up.

One might wonder why we were so eager to climb all the way to the top of the ladder when it was so dangerous. Well, there are two answers. Firstly, the danger was there, and the whole task was very risky. Kids did it for the thrill of it. Kids did it to show that they were manly and brave. Secondly, the view at the top was spectacular, especially at sunset and at sunrise. The orphanage seemed to be on a mountain or something, so it looked down seemingly upon the rolling hills below. The whole area was covered thickly by trees, and then villages seemed dotted sparsely throughout. So, when the sun rose or set, the whole view looked beautiful, like a pretty painting that seems only to be in fairy tales or something. It was really quite beautiful, something that took our breaths away. Also, at night time, the sky was extremely clear and filled with stars. I thought that each star was an eye of God, so that God could see everything all at once. When stars twinkled, I thought God was happy, like when you give someone a wink, as if to say "Yeah, it's me. Watch this!"

That's about all I remember of this place except that one incident that had us all move out of the orphanage. That was when the brick wall either fell down or someone tore a huge hole into it. I'm not particularly sure what really happened. The wall went down and a massive gap appeared. I couldn't imagine where anyone could get the axes and materials enough to tear down the wall. All I know is that one day I awoke and heard a lot of commotion. So, I ran outside and found that the left side of the orphanage wall had a huge torn hole in it. Almost all the kids were running out. There was a lot of chaos. It was actually thrilling, watching how the kids were trying to escape and the caretakers were trying desperately to catch them. The whole thing was a disaster. The moment the kids saw a way to run, they booked it like it was paradise. Remember that all these kids were way older; they probably knew how to live on their own. They probably hated the orphanage way worse than I did and realized quickly that they could live on the streets better than in an orphanage. They probably had in mind to run away and all of them to meet up somewhere down the road, maybe at the bottom of the big hill. Whatever it was, the big run was certainly a caretaker's worst nightmare. They are in charge of caring for government kids, homeless kids, paupers, and orphans alike. If the government showed up, which they do at least every six months or so for inspection, and they found out that a truckload of kids had ran away, the caretakers would lose their jobs and possibly go to prison. This was bad, and everyone knew it. I could tell from almost all of their faces that they were all wrecked and felt ruined.

Only a few, including myself, did not run. I almost did, but one of the caretakers had grabbed me before I even had my mind made up on what to do. There were at least about 10 kids who did not run, all of them exclusively young. We were all locked in room, where transportation was coming for another "relocation". We probably were in that orphanage barely a month. It had been alright. I don't remember being treated that badly, although I still got beaten a lot. However, it was an almost all older kid orphanage, so most of them were independent. But, since they all ran, and the wall couldn't be repaired, the ones left behind were to move to more contained places. And so the fourth orphanage was the most brief and interesting thus far.

PART THE FIFTH

Casa Doi and the First Few Months

Instead of a bus, we actually got a little van to drive us back to Bucharest. The driver was actually pretty nice, and I would know him well in time. He came quite fast, and we were loaded in the van like prisoners, our names being called repeatedly so as if to ensure that we hadn't disappeared in a blink of an eye. The bus driver was ordered to lock all the doors, which he did, and was given the instructions to never open any windows. That being done, we rolled out into the dusty roads really fast. The driver put some music on, and rolled down the windows regardless of the constant previous warnings. Everyone was pretty talkative through the ride, discussing everything that had happened, spitting out everyone's personal idea or opinion on what had happened or why it happened. I think everyone was just as clueless as I, though. Nobody really knew, although some of the kids suspected that one of the older kids had used a bomb to blow a hole in the wall. Another kid stated that God probably tore down the wall because He didn't like the orphanage better than anyone else did. That idea was actually pretty solid and explanatory for everyone; no one disputed it.

Anyhow, we neared Bucharest about mid-day. Once again, I saw the big Arch of Triumph looming up ahead and I already knew that the orphanage was nearby there. It was. We went through a gate into the same area the "Orphanage in the Middle of the Street" had been. However, we didn't go there. We went way back to where there was a smaller orphanage, one that could probably hold about 30 kids or so; maybe a little more. This orphanage was to be later known as Casa Doi, or "House Two". I am not sure why. I'm not quite aware how names were given out, but there were about three to five more orphanages in the area and our orphanage was Casa Doi. Pretty plain. Pretty simple.

Inside, the place looked bare and unhospitable. There were several big rooms upstairs. There was the common room, where the T.V. was; there were the two big dorms, dividing girls and boys; there was the "teaching" room, which I shall come to later; there was the eating room; the play room; the bathrooms; the hallway room; and finally, there were three little rooms-the "boss's" room, the caretakers' room, and the nurse's office. I don't remember what downstairs looked like-only very briefly. I'll mention it later in this memoir.

The first day, new kids came in, got dumped on the doorsteps of the orphanage, and pretty much got left there. I can say that most of these kids would be the ones I would know till the day I left Romania. Ionut had come back. He gave me a stupid grin and told me that he went up north. He introduced me to his two new friends, Roberto and a boy named Jeppa (this is the best way I can pronounce his name in the English language). Both of these kids would come to be my friends as well. Roberto was a popular kid who was very social and outgoing. Jeppa was a remarkably smart kid with an attitude of a know-it-all and a person that's been through everything. I also met a girl named Helga. She was a bight girl, one that went along with whatever came. She would later get adopted by American parents like me. The other kids I don't remember, although there is some I recall their personalities rather clearly, and comically.

We got a whole new set of caretakers. Some were to be alright while others ended up being vicious, vindictive, and almost pure evil. We met the caretakers at the doorstep. Since almost everyone was new, we were all given a tour of the orphanage, which was brief and to the point. It was made clear that there was a lot of repairs that needed to have been done and that in a year or so, the whole building was to be made into an orphanage for babies. So, that gave everyone a heads up that we weren't going to stay there but maybe a year or so. For now, it was winter time. Already the cold kicked in. Our beds upstairs still contained no pillows or blankets, but somehow, we managed to stay warm.

My whole life as an orphan would change very quickly. Firstly, we got a "boss" lady. Yes, the woman in charge of the orphanage. We would all call her the "boss lady' because she walked around in a suit and acted all preppy, like a lady, and was seemingly arrogant and snub all the time. We all absolutely hated her. The irony of all this was the acknowledgement that she had a lot of money. So, this being known, the caretakers were being paid more. Which meant they worried about their jobs more. Which meant that we would get beaten more. Which meant that we would go public more, and do more things outside in the world. Which meant that my lifestyle changed drastically.

Firstly, we all had new clothes to wear. More uncomfortable ones. Our socks were long and were like women's tights. Our shoes were Velcro. Our clothes were more western, and we then had to switch them out every so often. Everyone's heads were shaved out, so as to prevent lice. This happened every so often, like every 3 months or so. We were taken to the nearby huge church, which was the Casin Monastery, and baptized. Also, some of the kids, including myself, were enrolled into prep school. We were taught how to have better manners, such as to not spill out food on the table and to not pick up our bowls and drink out of them (although I still did). We had more television to watch, so we were better informed about the news and what happened in the world. And finally, we went on way more social outings.

Casa Doi, however, was not as good of an orphanage as I've just stated, though. Places and environments can have more open opportunities. However, that doesn't mean that situations improve. In fact, they could just become worse and more complicated. Casa Doi was such an orphanage. It was both interesting and eventful, but also confusing and complicated. In the end, I actually came out worse than I went in.

PART THE SIXTH

Where I Went to School and Had First Christmas

It must have been early fall when I went in the orphanage. We stayed inside a lot, listening to the stories some of the caretakers told us. There is only one story I really remembered well from these times stuck inside. Outside of our orphanage were cherry trees. They actually produced some really nice cherries. However, when it got cold, the tree seemed to dry up and didn't produce cherries no more. So, I was curious about this and I asked one of the caretakers why this happened. She told me that each tree had a beautiful lady inside of it. Every winter, the lady would die. The caretaker didn't explain why the lady would die, I just knew that she did. When the lady died, then everything around her would die as well. And like meat stays fresh when it's cold, the world would become cold and icy so that the tree would be preserved into spring. And then, the caretaker said, God would cry. I asked the caretaker why God would cry, and she would tell me that God holds his tears until the end of the year, where then he would just unleash all of his stored tears and make it fall onto the world as rain. And the rain would fall and melt the ice. And it would magically bring back to life the lady in the trees. And so the lady would be alive again and she would make the trees grow cherries again. This is the only story I remember that caretaker telling me.

Anyhow, around that time I was enrolled in prep school. The school was interesting because it actually had breakfast snacks and nap time in the middle of the day. Ionut and I were enrolled into a prep school nearby. We would often shock and surprise everyone because we would go around to each classroom asking for the breakfast snacks (which was usually bread and jam) because we were always hungry. We would often get into a lot of trouble. The schools were interesting. They offered no writing courses for Ionut and me, although they taught us how to be playful and active. We did a lot of physical education, learning how to do track and play indoor sports. We learned how to make crafts, like paper cups, hanging paper graffiti, and posters. We encountered and played with animals, like bunnies. We were read to a lot of stories; one I particularly remember being Stuart Little. We took naps in the middle of the day by pulling the beds constructed in the walls. Everything in the classroom was decorated and pretty. It seemed the school really wanted to make going there a wonderful place to be. I know the teachers were nice. I still did not learn to read or write. More focus went into learning how to paint, make crafts, play around in the gym, and learn how to sing and say the national anthem every morning.

After school was the best part. Then, we would all go around and make fun of everyone. I interacted with a lot of kids, who would play with me on the merry-go-rounds until their parents would come and scold them for playing with me. So, we would always have a look out, telling each other when the parents would come when. Outside, I would often smooch off of the other kids for food and candy. And they would give it to me out of kindness and probably pity. They were all good kids, kindhearted and well-meaning. They talked to me endlessly, telling me about what their typical lives were like but most wondering and questioning what it must be like as an orphan. It was a new concept to them, one that was most fascinating. However, they felt sorry for me, and ended up bringing more candies and food just to make me happy. I was O.K. with this at first. I would not be by the end of the stay there in Bucharest, though. I will go more into that later though.

I can certainly say that Christmas came quickly. It is actually the first one I remember. It wasn't remarkable, because no one had given me any presents nor anything special occur that day. I remember only hearing the song "Silent Night" playing from the nearby different colored beeping Christmas tree while I was sleeping and thinking to myself that it was the most beautiful song I've ever heard. It put me in a mood of peace and happiness. It was kind of like a striking moment when I thought that, for a moment, everything was going to be O.K. I had heard about the "Little Match Girl" story at school, where in the end, after being so cold and miserable, her grandmother carried her up to heaven and all the sudden, despite the cold and stings around her she felt a "warm presence". I never understood what that meant for the longest time. I could not fathom how a person could be cold and warm at the same time. But when I heard that song play on Christmas Day, I felt happy even though I was miserable living where I was at. The feeling lasted only for the night, but the song is just as special to me as it was when I first heard it. And even to the present day, with all the variety of music the world has produced, "Silent Night, Holy Night" is my favorite song ever.

PART THE SEVENTH

Roberto, Jeppa, Ionut, and Helga

Helga, Roberto, Jeppa, and Ionut became my best friends in the orphanage. They all had something that seemed to make them likable. Helga and I would become better friends once we both found out that we would go to America. That was later though. Roberto was my competition in many ways, because he had a cute face and all the girls and caretakers loved him. He gave me a desire to always try to one up him, so we had a sibling-rivalry situation, where I talked trash on him all the time and liked hanging around him the majority of the time not spent hating him. However, it seems that we had a subconscious agreement that it was better working the way we were with each other than to be apart and not care what the other did. Most of time it seemed that we spent everything in a bitter power struggle. Jeppa was incredibly smart. You couldn't say anything more. He was a coward, but he did know what he was talking about the majority of the time. He and I became good friends because he liked Roberto. So I assumed that whomever was a good friend of Roberto was a good friend of mine. Jeppa was Roberto's best friend and Ionut was my best friend. Although there was a big split in the middle, we were all friends of the same clique. Ionut was pretty daring, for he liked a lot of thrills, and managed to encourage me to try a lot of new things that enabled me to survive the orphanage with a completely different attitude. Of the group of four, Roberto and Ionut were definitely the core leaders. Jeppa and I just followed, sometimes putting our two cents in but really just taking what both Roberto and Ionut said and did as fact and the right way to do anything.

We slept together, doing practically almost everything together. We four stood out in Casa Doi for two reasons. The first related to Ionut and me. We were both troublemakers. For some odd reason, we couldn't stop messing up and not following rules. We were always doing stupid things like sneaking out late at night, making loud noises, annoying the living crap out of the kids and caretakers, demanding things and being arrogant, being defiant and rebellious, and refusing to be told what to do-unless we were getting a lot of beatings. Ionut and I never disagreed on what we did or downplayed the other. This way, it was almost impossible for other people to try to influence us and our decisions. Also, it was way easier because by agreeing with each other, we felt we weren't so accountable for our actions because both of us had done it. It would be hard to imagine myself doing anything if Ionut wasn't there to encourage me to do it. And vice versa. So, we depended on each other a lot. I can say that I trusted him a lot-in a very superficial way. We both realized that we were selfish people, and we both kind of accepted the fact that if a situation arose where one of us was going to get screwed over, than we both knew one of us was going to be selfish and let the other take the blame. We both knew this was how things were going to go. We shared our secrets, but our deepest secrets we kept to ourselves. We both weren't stupid enough to reveal anything to each other that might help the other take advantage of one of us. However, the way things worked was pretty solid. And that enabled us to have a lot of control in the orphanage, sometimes being solely responsible for the actions the orphanage as a whole committed a certain day.

That brings us to reason two. While Ionut and I were the troublemakers of the orphanage, Roberto and Jeppa were the angels of the orphanage. I have to pause and specify that Roberto and Jeppa weren't actually good, kind-hearted people, but that they were master manipulators. They acted good around the caretakers and thus enabled themselves to have favor with them. So they got their way a lot, by sucking up to the people that ran the orphanage. So, the other orphans would try to win Roberto's or Jeppa's favor by following them and doing what they wanted to do so that they could possibly get what they wanted. This was an ironic way of doing things, as Ionut and I were complete opposites form the other two. When we were told no, we did it anyway- with defiance and stubbornness. When they were told no, they tried to suck up and wish-wash their way through. A lot of the times they were successful, probably because they had such a likable personality. So, they stood out and we stood out. So, we ended up as the biggest influencers of the house. If the other kids wanted something, they'd go to Roberto and Jeppa and ask them to convince the caretakers to agree to it. Always that required the kid to do a service, but sometimes it seemed worth it, especially when they were getting ready to be beaten and needed someone to plead for their case. However, Roberto and Jeppa had a little more influence because the caretakers would have them tattletale or snitch on the others so they could get punished. To have that power to tell on someone and have them get punished for it because the caretakers take your word for it was pretty big. Thus, almost everyone did not try to mess with them at all.

Obviously, the snitching was a no-go for me and Ionut. In fact, I remember discussing with Ionut the idea that Jeppa and Roberto could no longer be friends with us because we were going to be snitched on all the time. Very early it looked like it would come down to that. So both of us would piss off everyone so much that we were getting beaten repeatedly. We ended up framing the other two, which ended up with both of them getting beaten and much of their influence diminished. Thus, the orphanage would then sway our side and we would end up being the top influencers. One of the perks we had was pissing off the caretakers so much that they would forget to beat the other kids and try to go after us. And I'm almost sure nobody liked the caretakers, so it was easy to see why we were so popular with the other kids. However, Roberto and Jeppa had another side to them. There's only so much sway words can have on stubborn caretakers. They wanted to do things that were not going to be approved by the ladies. So, they reduced their snitching-using it more as a threat than anything-and went about acting as normal orphans do, breaking rules and trying to have fun.

Thus it can be said that Roberto, Jeppa, Ionut, and I had the biggest influence in the house because of our personalities and actions. We all worked together to get what we wanted, and we all got the respect and acknowledgement of the others that we were leaders. Our influence extended to a point that Ionut could tell someone to do something and they would go do it. It was almost an everyday thing where someone would get in trouble and, when asked why they did it, they would respond that "Ionut and Nicu told me to do it" or "Roberto said so" and things like that. Obviously, we were scapegoats, but it also undermined the others' accountability because they all recognized that by listening to us, we had a lot of influence on what they did. At least that's what Jeppa told me. This dynamic way of doing things is a good reason why I became very well aware of social dynamics and structures. I was participating in them and structuring them at the same time. Even in such low places as orphanages, I was aware how my behavior was causing others to act.

Helga was way on the other spectrum. She was the most likable girl for reasons I can't really describe. She was easy to get along with, and she was very kind. She acted, one might say, like a royal princess. She did everything with grace, and all the caretakers loved her for it. She would get all their affections, and the best of what could be offered. Obviously, Helga did not care for anything other than getting hurt. She tried to avoid any situation that might lead her on a bad side with the caretakers. She definitely could wing pitifulness for she could cry almost on demand with amazing accuracy. She became the main "boss lady's" most likable orphan-a feat that would raise many caretakers' eyebrows-and thus wield almost incredible power amidst the caretakers themselves. After all, nobody wanted to piss off the "boss lady's precious little girl". That might end badly. So Helga stood out. I know for a fact that behind that sly smile was a real big grin that she could just ask anyone of anything and she would get it. She was good about that not going to her head-which made her that much more likable-but she would get irritated if people didn't recognize her special position as a special girl. If anything, besides the "boss lady", she definitely held the status as the queen of the house. Nobody wanted to piss her off.

I'm not really sure why Helga liked me. I know I was the first one to piss her off, to get severe beatings for doing so, and for beating the living shit out of her for it (which ended up with more beatings). I know the first few months in Casa Doi was the roughest because we both seemed to dislike each other. However, Helga went to school with me and seems to have been in almost every class I've ever been to as well as being the only other person to get adopted to America besides me. We spent a lot of time together, whether we wanted to or not, and it seems that our good interactions with each other made ourselves likable. Thus, later we became good friends and that enabled me to have more of a sway on her than any other person. I can say that if it hadn't been for Helga, I wouldn't have done so many things in Casa Doi that I wouldn't have had the privilege otherwise. It is the irony of the situation that Helga was an exception to the rule: I was able to access more opportunities and have more privilege through a girl than any boy or man. This is the case because in the orphanages, women ran everything and held all the power. Us boys were completely irrelevant to them.

PART THE EIGHT

Whereas I Learn to Believe the Orthodox Religion

Romania is, or rather was, a very strong religious country. I saw this more in the countryside, but it was also strong in Bucharest. One day I was sitting by the window playing my stupid snowflake game-counting how many snowflakes there was-when I saw a sister or nun below walking to our orphanage. She was holding a bag and some wooden sticks. Down below, she was welcomed in with respect, as all religious people are, and escorted upstairs where we were notified that this lady was going to teach us about God. So there we were, sitting there Indian style, listening to her telling boring bible stories. It was clear nobody cared about God, for He obviously didn't seem to be helping us out at the present moment. But the nun continued, using the wooden sticks to paste a woolen cover where she would take other woolen bible figures and stick them on the wool. Thus, she went step by step in describing the bible stories by moving the woolen figures on the white wool cloth so that they corresponded to the stories she was telling us. Needless to say, she became a regular visitor to our orphanage.

At first, I didn't care. All I did care about was whether she had brought candy, which she often did. For that, I tried to listen. However, I was definitely one of those people that couldn't comprehend religion because it wasn't very logical. I had already developed my ideas about God. God was very good. He felt sorry for people so He sent His son to the world to die. God also liked doves. God ruled Earth and everything around Earth. God protected Romania. God died to save people, but that was hard for me to understand, especially since I couldn't grasp how a dead person comes to life again. And anyway, how does dying save people? It was difficult for me to wrap my mind around this idea. Probably the biggest thing that I believed in was that God caused luck and that anytime you got hurt, God made you get hurt because you did something bad or you did something to piss Him off. The religious lady taught us that we each had a guardian angel, but that kind of freaked me out because then she told me that God and my guardian angel knew everything about me-my thoughts, my feelings, when I was planning to cheat and lie, all that. Now that's creepy, knowing someone else knows everything about you. Thinking about it more closely, I assumed I was a pretty bad person, that I would grow up bad, be bad, die bad, and go to hell bad. It would be a miracle if I went to heaven, I thought, but I was sure I was born bad, thus I would go to hell. And apparently, I heard, it's extremely hard to reach heaven, the road being narrow and all. The road obviously had to be really narrow because I sure as hell couldn't find it. I just assumed that if God wanted me to go to heaven, He'd make magical stairs that go from earth to heaven like that one story in the Bible. Other than that, I didn't put much thought into religion. I was already going at a bad direction anyway.

Thus, there remain my ideology of God and His Church. God was great. I was small. I acknowledged God and who He was, and I would just be in the corner not important at all. I was okay with this, because I didn't expect myself to ever achieve anything. I knew right from wrong, that wasn't an issue. I knew it was wrong to steal and lie. It is a basic instinct, because everyone knows when they're giving false information to someone when the other person wants the truth. It was just a matter of care. I didn't care to do the right thing because I already believed I was a lost cause. And I believed I was too insignificant for God to care that I cared. Whenever I went into the churches of Bucharest, I was truly humbled. I could feel that I was in a special place where God is great. The churches had a way of making you feel small, and it made me uncomfortable being in the presence of a great being. I felt I didn't belong because I was such a bad person. And if I felt like that in a church, imagine how bad I would feel if I'd been in the presence of God Himself! Really, I was okay with going to hell. I'd rather suffer in a place where I feel I belong than live in heaven in shame and humiliation. So I got the concept that only worthy good people go to church (and thus heaven) and bad unworthy people stay away and keep to themselves.

Sometimes I would try to be nice, just to feel what this must be like. Trying to model myself to how Helga was, I tried to be kind if I had more than enough for me and another person. I did think about being respectful, calling people by saying "Sir" or "Madame". I tried to be really generous, a trait that would stick with me as I got older, because I knew other people didn't have a lot of stuff sometimes. I was empathetic to people, even though those people were people I liked. Although I had little awareness or care how people thought or felt about me, I definitely tried to help those whose image was scarred or demented. I didn't care or judge people, unless they were Russians, because I was taught that you should always be cautious of Russians and their manipulative tactics. I was very honest, to the point where I was rude about it. I stated exactly how I felt, and I didn't sugar coat anything when it came to preference of anything. I respected old people a lot, because they seemed to be safe and wise. They seemed to have grown out of things like sex, drinking, thinking stupid, trying new things, being worried constantly, and everything else that comes when you reach manhood. They went with the flow and told you things that were useful. I tried to treat girls with respect but I just couldn't shake the idea that girls were just people that looked pretty, were extremely annoying and difficult, and had pigtails for me to yank. Yanking pigtails was actually addicting for me, mainly because I thought it was so comical when the girls would scream and get so mad. Then I would get slapped in the face and I would burn with desire to pull their pigtails that much harder next time, just to get back at them.

I had my good qualities mixed up in such a way that they don't seem very good. But I did have qualities that would shine a little, that separated me from a thin line between a demon and a human kid. However, I can say my good qualities were very slim. I acted out of expression, trying to mimic the behaviors of the others that I admired, like Helga and Ionut. They were all older than me, and they seemed to have everything together. It was difficult finding my own identity because I got too many confusing messages across the board. The religious lady told to act holy and godly. But the caretakers didn't. Ionut, Jeppa, Roberto, and the "boss lady" didn't. By acting good, I was making myself more vulnerable to getting screwed over and get taken advantage of. By acting bad, I could get what I wanted and nobody would expect anything else. Everyone would expect I was a loser, that I wasn't going to go anywhere, and thus they would leave me alone. That way, I was happy and I didn't have to try very hard. Plain and simple. Easy way out. Being good is definitely hard work. Whereas being bad, well; you can swing on someone if you don't like them.

There was a lot of religious people that would come and do charity work at Casa Doi. They would put on plays about the Bible and give us toys. The best present I ever received was a big yellow truck that I would play with all the time outside in the sand by the junkyard. The people would make us food and teach us how to play games. Although these were good times, I don't remember them very much, due to the fact that I started realizing that people were giving me stuff because they felt sorry for me. It was a pivotal moment for me, when I realized my condition as an orphan meant a social status, that being at the very bottom of the grand scale. It also was the first time I questioned myself, wondering why I had become an orphan in the first place. It sparked an annoying idea in my head, that perhaps my mother did not like me, that I wasn't wanted, that I was unmanageable. Perhaps that's why everyone pitied me and gave me candy and toys. After all, you can just imagine what goes through their minds when you look at their concerned faces and outstretched arms. These thoughts would boggle my mind, and it caused me great mental discomfort. It was hard to fathom why I wasn't wanted.

PART THE NINTH

Whereas I Encounter Beautiful Gardens and Beautiful Days

In time, the winter turned into spring. Whereas the winter was brutal and cold, gray and stinging with biting shock, the spring came almost blooming. The cherry tree burst into cherries. Flowers grew everywhere. Everything became lush and green. Stray dogs that huddled under the orphanages now seemed to stroll the streets with an air of confidence. We woke up to the sounds of birds chirping, which were amazing timekeepers because they all seemed to start chirping around 5 o'clock in the morning, almost to an accurate timing. Cars congested the city streets like never before, so that up above, we would sit by the window and make faces at the drivers below. People walked on the streets by the dozens. Pretty much what happened was that the whole city of Bucharest seemed to wake up and start living.

Needless to say, we went to the park a lot. By us, there was a garden up just by our orphanage. It was spectacularly beautiful, for it had streams and waterfalls, flowers that looked exotic, and lush trees everywhere, drooping down its branches until it reached the water below. I remember vividly how I would go to the bushes and pick the berries, until I was stuffed with them. I was doing this one day when I accidentally slipped and fell into a certain bush. I crashed right into a big hollow space. Now, this was absolutely incredible to me, for it was a medium size tree, not very outstanding. All its branches folded out into a semi-circle, and the branches just drooped from the top to make a hollow space. But the tree was surrounded by bushes and other big trees, so that the hollow space was literally invisible to anyone looking in. But I could look out clearly and see everything beyond me. It was amazing, and I had to show Ionut. He thought the place so ingenious that from then on, whenever we played hide and seek or whenever we sneaked out of the orphanage, we would hide there. It became our fort and hideout, where we could store things and ensure nobody would find it. The place, which we termed "the cave", was so secluded in the bushes that for a while we got lost trying to find it again.

Outside the hallowed space was just fountains and rows upon rows of flowers that seemed to stretch out endlessly. It was remarkably beautiful, although everyone took it for granted because we saw it every day. There were roads leading to the gardens that were surrounded by lush tall trees, so that the sunlight came through the cracks like streams of magical rays. The trees were amazing because they seemed to bend toward each other so that the road seemed to be barreled in. We would play soldier all the time on those roads, because there would be so many people that would come through there, either by walking, biking, or skating. I tell you, I'm not a flower or tree person, nor do I care much about biology. But the gardens were beautiful, especially early in the morning, where the guards would open the gates and I would feel like I stepped into a Peter Pan fairy tale, where fairies where real and mermaids lurked in the clear waters below.

We encountered so many people. Lots of lovers, lots of kids, lots of people on cellphones, lots of people who picnicked, lots of people that skated, lots of people that played on their Gameboys, lots of people that seemed to just enjoy the gardens, lots of pretty girls, lots of gawking boys, and us orphans. Everyone and everything seemed to be there. It was a favorite spot for a lot of people to go to, and it was the only time we kids had the liberty to be told "go play" and we gladly sped off to whatever we did and come back hours later. The gardens in Bucharest were one of my happiest memories as a kid living in Romania.

PART THE TENTH

Whereas I Encounter an Old Lady and Get My Baptism and First Communion

Around the same time that we were going to the parks, I tore my already worn-out shoes to shreds. So, I was told to take them downstairs to a room where an old lady worked. So, I went down and went through the miserable looking place, which was filled with junk: old books, old toys, countless shredded clothes and socks, old shoes, everything. It was as if an orphan holocaust occurred and all the kids were stripped of their belongings, and their stuff was just dumped downstairs. It became clear to me why nobody went down there. Anyway, I finally squeezed through and went into a little room that smelled of oil and licorice. And hunched over in a little corner was an old lady, working away at something I completely forgot as time went by. She was so busy working at whatever she was doing that she did not notice me. I pounded the door very politely and even coughed gently, but she still didn't respond. So, I just said "hey" and went on to explain that my shoes were torn. She looked up then, and then looked at me, and I swore I jumped three feet backwards. She was so old and hideous, so scary looking. I was got off guard. I had in mind to just drop the shoes and go barefoot forevermore, but she smiled at me and motioned for me to give her my shoes. So I did, and I stood silently behind her, trying to catch my breath.

I looked around the room. It was pretty spectacular. All these gadgets, wheels, dangerous looking equipment. But everywhere I turned, there were clocks and watches, hundreds of them, all ticking, all systematically with the same timing. It was remarkable. The lady had been watching me as I had looked the room over, and seemed to see my interest in all the watches and clocks that were there. She asked me politely if I'd like to know how the clocks worked, whereas I was curious and responded in a positive note. So, the lady took one of the clocks down from a corner, and showed me all the intricate gadgets the clock had in order for it to work. I was so enthralled over this amazing thing that I spent all day observing this lady tell me everything there was to know about clocks. To the point where my shoes remained shredded and I didn't really care. The old lady ended up being a remarkably hideous person. From that day on, I saw this lady in her little office every day, or as nearly as I could. I found out that besides her usual task of being a tinker, she was actually the orphanage's cook and laundry cleaner.

There, I would sit on her lap and try fixing the clocks myself, trying to fit everything together. I would listen to her tell me stories while eating licorice, which happened to be her favorite thing to eat. She told me the story of "Pinocchio". Not the Disney one, the actual Italian story by Carlo Collodi. Besides "Peter Pan" by Barrie, Collodi's story became my favorite story ever. I was fascinated by all the metaphors and adventures, but most especially the Blue Fairy. I thought that there would be nothing more wonderful than having the Blue Fairy as my mother. I would dream about her and be all sad that she seemed so far away and unreal. When I grew up, and I saw the movie "Artificial Intelligence" and saw the kid try to find the Blue Fairy, boy, I could relate to that so much. It's as if I had always wanted a mother-a good mother, one that holds you and has a beautiful warm smile-and not be so alone and miserable. The old lady seemed to create in me a desire to learn so much more, because she knew so much. She answered my questions and helped me with any problems I might have had. She was a really good person to me, even though I must have pestered her a lot. I never knew her name, for I just called her the old lady and nothing more. I remember her strictly for the fairy tale stories she told me, especially the Hans Anderson ones, and the clocks and licorice. She fixed my shoes, but I went barefoot anyway.

Finally, one day, I think it was Easter or so (it was on a very religious holiday), all of us orphans were rounded up and were told to wear nice clothes. Besides the nice clothes, which nobody had to wear, we went outside and went to Casin Church in Bucharest. It couldn't have been that far away because we actually walked there. The church was located some stairs high (for you had to climb the stairs to get to the church). Inside was spectacular, covered in bright colors. Old people were in the church, hunching in the seats on the wall, giving us empathetic smiles and watching us as we were told to be silent and reverent because we were in a place of God. Not that we needed a heads up or anything-all of us could see that.

The walls were high, and almost everything was covered with bright colors or golden metal. There was incense everywhere and it nearly choked the living breath out of me. A service was held, with all the people behind us, and the water was blessed, whereas one by one, each kid was immersed in the water three times before being dried and moved on to the other people who broke a piece of bread and had you eat it and the next guy who served you wine on a spoon. It was a long ritual, for there must have been about forty of us. Ionut and I were in the back, as we were different and not so liked. The Communion ceremony was interesting and amazing. I felt very special, like I was being initiated into a secret society, like the Freemasons or the Illuminati. I felt like I belonged and I was just observing an exotic ritual that could turn out all wrong if you said anything stupid. But of course, I was in a house of God and I felt highly uncomfortable. I wasn't so sure water would erase all my sins and that I would be given a new life. I didn't feel anything strange when I arose from the water, other than I almost drowned and didn't close my mouth when the priest pushed me in the water. It was too confusing to take in, so I just let it happen. The Communion was different, for eating bread and drinking wine that's supposed be the body and blood of God seemed more like cannibalism to me than anything else. The wine was especially unique because I felt a fire sensation in my body after I drank it from the spoon.

After the whole incident, we all went outside and waited while all the people in the church came out and gave us bread and wine. We went back to the orphanage pretty quiet, not knowing what was so important after what just happened and thinking it was just another thing that happened in life. Nobody considered the idea that baptism and communion is very important to Romanians. But then again, nobody really listened to the people that came to tell us that.

PART THE ELEVENTH

Whereas I Recall the Central Playground, the Peculiar Tree Stump, the Junkyard, and the Back Roads

Outside our orphanage there was a playground. It was surrounded by a fence and it was pretty small. All the orphanages around us had playgrounds, but only two actually stood out. There was one by the orphanage in the middle of the street, the one where we would have had our "battles", and the one just across Casa Doi. That one had a swimming pool and a huge tree that seemed to loom over everything. Also, behind the tree and the sandy area was a junkyard.

The playground across Casa Doi actually belonged to the orphanage across us. That orphanage was much bigger and had more orphans, but it was difficult to keep us separated. The more people you have to play, the better. Everybody knew that. So, whenever they were out, we went to play with them. It's hard to say what we actually did, because I don't remember much of it. I do remember playing on the swings and trying to see who could fly out the farthest. Also, I remember going through the junkyard a lot to find out all the interesting things that might in there. I would find a lot of needles and metal car parts, and I would try to put these together to make something. That was what I did a majority of my time-try to put random pieces of junk together and make something. Other than that, I would explore a lot. Under the orphanages, stray dogs would make their homes, so I was curious what else was down there. I was more than surprised to find cubs, and I took a fascination with trying to teach the little dogs how to do tricks. They would respond pretty well if there was food, until one of the dogs bit me when I tried picking up one of the dogs. Then I did not mess with the dogs, for they took it pretty personal when I tried interacting with their young.

By the orphanage across Casa Doi, there was a little patch of ground that had radishes and roses. I used to pluck the radishes up from the ground when I was most hungry, and it was a good way of me to have food around without anyone knowing it was by us. While exploring, I found a ton of toys under the orphanage in the middle of the street. It was so full of past toys that it was impossible to take the toys out unless we shattered the basement windows and took the toys that way. One of the toys, that being a tricycle, we cleaned up and used it for a race later on. We also found tons of junk that was similar from what we would find in the junkyard. However, our discovery was short lived. The orphans of that orphanage got pissed off we were using "their toys" and we ended up getting beaten for messing around, being nosy, and playing with filthy toys.

One day, the big tree across our orphanage had a huge branch fall off due to some strong winds. So, some people came and cut it down, which left a huge round stump right in the middle of the street. This wasn't very spectacular other than the fact that we used the stump to give speeches on. Almost always, whenever we all came outside, everyone gathered around the stump and discussed the latest news in their orphanage. Every now and then, when either Ionut or I had a scheme in the back of our minds, we would stand on the stump and spit out words and directions. The stump was particularly important for whomever had candy, because then they would take center stage and we would hold auctions for who would give out the most service for a single candy. The stump was also where some of the orphans would dance and show off their moves for the others, particularly when everyone would compete for who was the best singer. So, the stump served as a little stage.

The junkyard. Really smelly. Really dark. Really interesting. It served as a concrete wall between us and the other side. It was like a little rectangular long house that held just about anything that was no longer in use by anyone. I used to always dig in that thing for months upon months. Then I got bored, convinced that I saw and felt everything there was. So, I got this grand idea that I should just climb over the wall and see what's on the other side. Since I was small, this was really difficult to do, but I managed to get the others to help me up. So, I got on top of the junkyard building and looked over. Apparently, I had made a lot of commotion on my side, because here was an old man who looked both surprised and pissed at the same time. By the time we both laid eyes on each other, he had picked up something and thrown it at me, demanding I get down and leave his yard alone. I took one quick glance at his yard, which seemed enclosed and really dirty, before I jumped down on my side. However, later on other orphans tried to jump on the junkyard building and get to the other side, but there he was again, this time hollering and throwing scraps of metal at us, until we ended cursing him out and giving up the idea of trying to climb the wall and get to the other side.

The area that Casa Doi was in was part of a larger group of orphanages, none of whom I know the names of. This area was surrounded by several things. The main part, by the Arch, was surrounded by stone wall with iron stakes. In the back, where we were, the wall was a bunch of old train cabs. Across from us, the junkyard became that wall. Contained in this big thing of walls must have been at least six orphanages and dozens of ghost buildings, forgotten and filled with junk that nobody wanted.

Since we were all orphans, and thus orphanages, and we all did a lot of things together, we had to communicate a lot amongst ourselves. We weren't very lucky, as almost all the orphanages did not have phones other than the bosses, who were out of the offices most of the time and would never allow anyone to ever touch their phones unless it was specifically themselves. So, the way we got any word around was by sending out kids to deliver the news to and from the orphanages. Obviously, whomever the caretakers trusted the most would be couriers. Ironically, that's how it's supposed to be. But some days, going around delivering messages was an all-day job. Jeppa and Roberto were naturally picked from Casa Doi to be its couriers. Except that Jeppa was rather chubby and not physically fit. And Roberto socialized to the point that it was impossible to get any news quickly because he always stopped and wanted to talk, and he would always excuse himself by saying that all the other caretakers would keep him because they wanted to talk with him, which, in part, was true. So, because we were the swiftest and fastest kids in Casa Doi, Ionut and I became all the caretakers' couriers. That also had in part to do that the caretakers didn't want to deal with us any more than they had to.

Actually, this job was great for us. We went around everywhere, getting the latest gossip and meeting so many different people. We became acquainted with the lady that was in charge of the water in the area, for she was somewhat on the road to the other orphanages. She would show us the huge pipes in the big building she ran, where she had complete control how the water ran and who got it. It was pretty spectacular. Sometimes she would let us climb the pipes and try to climb our way to the top, which must have been at least three or four stories high. Also, we saw the big parking lot where there were buses. Here, we met a bus driver that would become a great guy because he took an interest in me and Helga and would give both of us candy. And so many more. I would feel so special and grown up when I went from orphanage to orphanage, having all the orphans stare at me and wonder what interesting news I brought that day. I felt special being able to be trusted with caretakers' personals traded from caretaker to caretaker as the day went on. If I was transporting money, Ionut would take out enough so that nobody noticed. The rest we would split amongst each other, and it would go as our school money, so that we didn't look so poor and have to go without food some days.

Being a courier was definitely one of the best jobs I had as a kid. I really enjoyed getting information from people and the running all the way to the other side of the whole area to relate that information to other people. The main reason, I think, I particularly enjoyed this was because I was entrusted with often times secret information. If, for example, staff was going to be replaced or orphans were going to leave, I would know first. Another thing was the planning of the outings. I would relay to the other orphanages what we were going to do that day, and would arrange to see if that orphanage wanted to go with us as a group. And so on. There were quite a lot of perks to being able to hold information and disclosing it when it was necessary.

Probably the greatest thing about this job was the fact that I had a small amount of liberty in making quick decisions for the staff. For example, if they sent me out with money, I would choose what to buy based on how much money I had- I just needed to get a particular item, but the details were left to me. For a seven-year-old, this ability made me feel very important and mature, and it may have nurtured my early desire for a career in diplomacy. After all, I didn't necessarily disclose all the information I was told to say. I simply selected what I felt was most suitable in that situation. I learned to manipulate better, essentially. And the respect and understanding of who we runners were and what we did was known throughout the whole area, even to the police guards who guarded the front gates leading into our area, who would often use us to relay information to the orphanages. That exclusive treatment fed my ego and made me feel extremely special.

PART THE TWELFTH

Whereas I Observe a Bicycle Race,
the Olympics of 2000, and the Danube River Trip

2000 A.D. was a somewhat great year. It was the second big thousand. Everybody said we were going to die. And there was the Olympics. And that one music commercial that would come on repeatedly, called "the memories", but I have no idea who sang it. It was just a great song to listen to. We kept up with the Olympics like Americans keep up with the Super Bowl. We rooted for Romania, hated the Russians, cheered Australia, Germany, and the United States of America. Lots of good commercials, lots of trash talk. I was amazed about the African American runner, whatever her name was, that seemed to outstrip anyone going against her. Her speed was remarkable, and I remember watching her run and wondering if she was even human. She seemed to zip past everybody and she made it look easy.

However, it was another important event that made me feel special. It was the bicycle race. Jeppa had said Bucharest was hosting a bicycle race at the park for kids, so that we should select someone to ride the tricycle and get a crew to help him out. Everyone immediately chose Roberto, because he was good with anything that required movement, and we got started polishing up a tricycle. We practiced a lot, Jeppa being really helpful and informative on the best way to gain the most speed and all. The old lady from downstairs did something to the bike so that when Roberto pedaled it, it would continue going for a few seconds more unless he braked it. The lady made the bike able to pick up speed with incredible ease, coming almost as fast as riding a regular bike. It was pretty cool. We rolled out finally a week later, to participate in the race, and to cheer Roberto on.

The day was nice, and the race was unfair. Roberto and another kid were the only ones with tricycles; everyone else had bicycles. It would be no match. But Roberto actually kept up his speed, and he managed to come in fourth place, which wasn't anything because he didn't win. However, he got so disgusted with the bike that he let me have it, and I took a stroll with Ionut around the parks and acted all cool (Roberto had let me borrow his broken sunglasses). It was an interesting scenario, and I enjoyed it a lot. Ionut and I traded out pedaling the bike, and we ended up just biking back to the orphanage. We got somewhat of a commotion because we were biking in the street and keeping up traffic, but it was a great day.

A little while later, all of us went on a river cruise, I'm assuming, by the Danube, because it's closest (and we actually got back that day). We took a nice breezy trip, which I don't remember anything of except the part where we got off the boat and they handed us bags of candy. I lost my bag and ended up stealing someone else's almost instinctively. This was important moment for me; it was the first time I actually felt sorry for the other person, because he was crying, wondering where his bag had gone. Now granted, I wanted to give the bag back to him, but then I knew I would look worse and probably have my eyes knocked out of me once the caretakers would find out. So I just went on, acting as if I didn't know what he was talking about. It was a catch 22. You can't be honest because you get in trouble. Some people say that if I didn't do wrong in the first place, I wouldn't have to tell on myself. I always get mad when people told me this. You see, it would never cross my mind that I had done anything wrong until after I had done it. Then, it's kind of pointless to do anything afterwards, because I would get the living shit beaten out of me. As an orphan, nobody really praises you for doing the right thing because everyone expects you to be bad. So, in reality, there was no point in trying to give that kid back his bag. Eventually, he was going to do the same thing to me anyway.

PART THE THIRTEENTH

Whereas I Discuss School

We moved school sometime after spring ended. We moved to a school by Casa Doi. I know this because Helga, Ionut, and I used to walk to the school all the time, often times accompanied by a really nice caretaker who would take us to the park after school let out. The school was situated within the limits of other buildings, kind of snuggled in. The only thing that distinguished it from the others was the fact that the school had an iron gate. The school itself was maybe three stories high, and it looked kind of crummy compared to the school I had been to previously.

At first, we used to walk to school. The days were nice. However, as summer was going, soon we had a driver take us to school. It was the same guy who drove us to Casa Doi from the previous orphanage. He was really quite cool, because we would always arrive at school early so he would drive us to the parks and let us play. Our caretaker who was in charge of supervising us must have been pretty to him because he was content to do whatever she asked. He seemed to be delighted having the 45 more minutes with us every morning and evening when he took us back to the orphanage. It was, however, his job to ensure we were safe and went to school on time. He would wait patiently for us every morning as we awkwardly put on our school uniforms and would patiently wait for us after school, even after we lingered to talk to classmates and teachers. He was definitely one to keep secrets, and he broke a lot of rules driving us wherever we might have wanted to go. He would bring a lot of candy for us, and good food his mother made for the caretaker. Sometimes we would picnic in the park if the day wasn't so hot and we were tired enough to sit and be still. He was like our father figure, telling us how to behave in public and what to say respectfully. He was actually one of the few people in my life that did not treat me like I was a stupid kid. His attitude was nonchalant, content with his job, happy with life, and very optimistic about everything. Granted, he was smart and wise, often dreamy like-in his own world. He said things that were profound, that made sense, and was there when I had difficult issues come up. He was a guy that I could trust but not really. The driver didn't press for us to have a relationship with him. He took his job seriously, but really did not interact with us. His main attention was the caregiver, whom he talked with endlessly and seemed highly infatuated with. Whatever the caregiver liked or seemed concerned about, he partook in that concern and agreed with her likes. And the caregiver happened to be quite a good, kindhearted person who did care about our wellbeing and that we went to school to learn. So, the driver was therefore concerned about us, ensuring we were at school the moment the gate opened.

To put simply, that school had to be the worst and best school ever. It was bad because Ionut and I had no money and good clothes to wear, so that we looked very different from the other kids. We got bullied and taunted a lot, to the point where there would be fights and bloody noses. We smelled awful, and we were made aware of how everyone hated us for it. We never had lunches because we had no money nor was our orphanage able to afford us having food for lunch (or maybe the "bosslady" wouldn't give us any food). If we were lucky, the nice caretaker would make some food for us, but that happened rarely. We stood out so much that I began to take notice and feel embarrassed and humiliated for who I was. I felt lonely and deprived, completely left out and singled out. Ionut and I had different classes, so it made it worse because we were left as the only kid in the classroom with colored skin and clearly orphans, which everyone knew. But nothing would be worse than the teachers. They hated us. Plain and simple. They didn't like us. They put us in the back of the rooms, in the already worn-out desks that were scratched and torn, solid and uncomfortable. They never called on us, no matter if we raised our hands or not. They acted like we didn't even exist. They demanded that we be like the other kids, dressing alike, talking alike, writing alike, drawing alike, singing alike, everything like the other students. They wouldn't tolerate us being poor and having to dig in the trash for pencils. She demanded we write with fountain pens, like all the others. They complained so much about it that the "boss lady" had to buy us the pens and ink, which was really expensive. The "boss lady" would blow up whenever we would run out of ink, which was every day, because then she would have to buy more. Getting a fill up every day was usually acquainted with the boxing of our ears and the smacking of our heads onto the wooden desk she worked at.

But the teachers wouldn't let up, always complaining about every little thing we did or didn't have. So, Ionut and I were made to do everything different. We had to take showers every morning. We got new uniforms, one for each day, the nice caretaker being in charge of making sure our clothes were washed and pressed (for our uniforms were ironed). Also, we got backpacks and school supplies, as good as all the other students. We would be made jam sandwiches and given hot milk for the lunch period. The "boss lady" even had lectured us on how to be proper, such as saying "sir" and to kiss a woman's hand when we first met them. We were told the proper way to walk, and given a strict warning to not screw up in public as there would be severe consequences if we did. It was explained by the "boss lady" that we not to make her look bad or she would beat us.

But school did not improve any better. Students still did not interact with us, unless it was recess and we played football. The teachers would not help us if we asked them for help, telling us with an air of disgust to find out ourselves the answer. It grew on me the fact that I didn't know much, and I was curious to know what everyone else knew. It was the first time I thought about the future and what it might hold for me. I realized that most likely, I was going to end up on the streets, dealing drugs and selling stolen products. Relevant to the outings Ionut and I would go on every night in the streets, I had a feeling that my livelihood was going to be in the underground, hiding from the police force and living dirty. I realized almost immediately that people didn't like my kind and that I wasn't very cute or handsome. Pretty soon, I knew, I would grow older. My voice would deepen. My boyish features would leave me and I would grow hairy and ugly, like the other kids I met on the streets. By then, I would have had to go on the streets and steal, snatching food and products right before people's eyes and running away as fast as possible.

I could have joined a gang of boys under the leadership of a boy who supposedly knew the "ways" of street life, but that was really risky. There were tons of gangs on the street, and having so many was more of a threat for each one of them, as then they would have to compete with resources. So, all the gangs hated each other. Pretty soon, somebody was going to get shot or somebody would report on the group and everyone would go to prison. Everyone was suspicious of the other, to the point that, if you weren't careful, you were done for. One click. Two clicks. Then you're a dead body in the sewers, with no one to mourn you or find out about you for a long long time. That may seem like an exaggeration, but I was depending on all the movies I saw in the orphanage plus what the kids would tell me to make up this image of what my life would become in the near future.

Needless to say, that's not what I wanted to be, although I did recognize and accept that this was going to become my life. After all, at 16, the orphanage kicked you out of the system and you were on your own. I became curious to learn, though, because I felt the world was an amazing thing. I liked learning about mountains and history. I liked spelling out words and writing. I felt like I was smart, because the orphans back at Casa Doi didn't know how to write or spell. I loved hearing about great warriors and leaders. I dreamed to be like them, loved by everyone, admired and exalted. To be great was my biggest dream. It didn't matter what kind of person that would mean-being the pope, the president of Romania, the best football player, the guy with the most money, the Secretary-General of the United Nations, anything. I just wanted people to look up and be proud of me-

and me to feel big and badass-and for me to leave a legacy as great as Caesar, Napoleon, Alexander the Great, and Vlad the Impaler. I wanted to be a legend, remembered forever. But I knew that I had to be smarter than everybody, and more knowledgeable about a lot of things. I wasn't stupid, I knew knowledge was the first step to power, being able to outdo the other person because you could think in ways that people admired. I mean, I knew I wasn't the best at sports, no matter how good I was. There was always going to be someone stronger, faster, and more athletic than me. And sometimes, your body can't do what another could. And there was nothing I could do about it. But learning, well, learning I could gain and grow by myself. And I knew that. That's why I asked a million questions. I wanted to know, curious to know. The fact that I didn't know consumed me, to the point where I would be mad and hate everybody.

So this was school. And it wasn't pleasant. But in all the world, I would never trade it. There was a great deal of things that school offered me, most notably a chance to play and participate with the other students. It was my first glimpse at what a normal childhood looked like, because I would observe parents picking up the students, or hear stories of the fun things the other kids did in their free time or on the weekends. I did not really speak about what happened in the orphanages, primarily because I clearly stood out in the classroom. I know that the teachers were aware, and that the other kids knew that I had no parents, but the whole idea of me vocalizing this was something I never considered. I listened to the other students and despised them for doing things I never could do. The biggest thing that school offered was the idea that I was special, because most of the other kids in the orphanage did not go. I was aware that I was going to school for a reason, but I never really understood the full reason why. I made up my own reasons, and that's how I liked it. School was just a badge that I wore, and nothing more. After all, in school, I was definitely an outsider, but back in the orphanage, I could make up anything about school because no one knew better.

PART THE FOURTEENTH

Whereas I Encounter My Adopted Family and Other Things

Now, our orphanage (or the orphanages) was surrounded by a big iron fence. At the front gate was stationed a police house. The house had maybe three or four police officers at one time. They weren't really relevant, other than the fact that they always had big black dogs with them. These dogs were part of the squad, too. They made sure that nobody ran or did anything suspicious. They were terrifying creatures, for they bit you if you ran. Their bites hurt quite a bit, and it was impossible to run away from them. I remember the dogs really well, because we kids would have a race and they would come running at us, scaring the crap out of us. We would run up the trees or stand very still until they ran away.

However, other than this terrible memory I shall never mention again, I shall casually move on to that big party at that playground. It was tremendous, just like the one the year before. Many people came, there was lots of music and food, we played many games, and all the while I remember the weather being really nice. I remember bobbing for apples, and the fact that no one told me how to act or yelled at me for anything. It was a nice day. It was an important day because, later, I noticed that the weather was changing and it was suddenly becoming colder.

Actually, the big pivotal moment was when I first encountered some strange people. There were some female workers who came to see me. They took me and Helga and a few others on an outing trip. I felt pretty lucky, considering that I was the only guy in the group being taken out by girls. They observed us while we played and acted stupid on the playground. I'm not sure how I came to understand it, but I eventually found out that I was being looked at for the possibility of adoption. Of course, I was young and had no idea what that meant or what it implicated, but the fact of the matter was, I was someone special, or else no one would choose to adopt me. If anything, my self-esteem went up and I felt like I was better than everyone else.

This was a big advantage to me in many ways, because whenever anything special happened at the orphanage, I claimed that my adopted family donated it. I used this lie to solidify the fact that they were rich and that because they were rich, I was rich, and everyone else was a loser to not be great enough to be selected for adoption. It is ironic because I was really becoming more arrogant around that time, feeling (for some unknown reason) that I was better than others in that good things happened to me because I was, in some way, special. There wasn't really any justification for why I was special. It had never occurred to me why I was special. I remember shrugging people off when they asked me why I thought I was special. I would just say something stupid, something that sounded quite similar to "Because, it's me". I just know that when good things did happen to me, it just justified my case (at least in my mind anyways). I remember that I used to respond very sarcastically when people asked me if I was special; I would smile and say *"asa si asa"* (so so). It is a phrase I never forgot.

It seems logical to think that this idea became rather questionable for some time, adopted family and all. The chances were rare for an orphan to be adopted (in fact, I don't even remember one person getting adopted other than Helga). It was becoming more of a recognized lie, so I was much relived when I was told one day when I was told that my adopted family had come to see me. I was very excited, and unsure of what to expect. Before, there was a woman named Ms. Debbie who had videotaped me eating some candy on the swing outside of the orphanage. She had told me to say hi to the video camera, but I was too stupid to understand what she was trying to do. I just smiled and crammed the candy in my mouth because I was fearful that she would take it from me (in fact, several times she did, so that I could smile in the camera). But now, I was going to meet this family who gave me candy that I always had to hide, and the candy, of course, that brought about so many fights because people stold them.

When I first saw this family, I didn't know what to make of them. There was a man, built and tall. There was a woman with fluffy hair (I didn't know that she was to be my mother, I thought she was a charity worker), and there was a girl. The girl was sick. I could see it in her eyes, the way she didn't respond to many things. I knew that because I saw that look many times in the orphanages from the other kids. She made me think that this family were some kind of charity people. Anyhow, there they were. They were very nice to me. They smiled a lot (too much, I thought). They liked to hug me a lot, which made me feel really uncomfortable. They took a photo, and even videotaped me again. It was the first time I felt a little shy, for I felt very awkward. I was getting candy, but I wasn't understanding that they were my adopted family. I guess I must have had another impression, not these smiley people who wanted to hug me all the time and be really close to me. I remember looking into the little girl's eyes and thinking that she looked very sick, and it made me think that she had a disease or something. She just had a bad air to her. But, the meeting went fast, and there was some problems with the video camera (I was quite fascinated with it), and I was escorted back to the orphanage with candy and the acknowledgment that they were the family that was going to adopt me. For me, I just couldn't believe it. I felt sincerely sure this was a joke of some sort, and went along feeling like this was a charity thing.

I hid the candy in the upstairs playroom, but the others found it, which resulted into a big fight. To the point where the door to that room (which had a window on it) was shattered and we all got into big trouble. I was not told that the adopted family was going to see me the next day. Many years later, I was told that they wanted to see me the next day, but that the staff had told them that I was crying too much (because I didn't want to leave them, I presume). I know that this was a lie, because my tears were not for the family any more than the beatings I was receiving for getting into a fight over the person I suspected stold my candy. However, it was typical for staff to smooth talk outside people in such a way that the other person felt good about themselves and suspected nothing bad was occurring in the orphanage.

However, that moment did solidify my stance that someone was going to adopt me. Hence, it gave me credit and when some bikes were magically donated to the orphanage, I immediately claimed that my adopted family was the one who donated them, making me the one who had the authority to "give" them out to others, which I promptly did. There was no real argument anyway, because I "gave" the bikes out to the ones who were going to take them anyway, regardless of what I said. The fact that they recognize that I "gifted" them something, though, made them feel that they needed to "gift" me something in the future.

And here, I become quite sketchy on where I went or did. Two really important things happened after this incident-the big Christmas part and the big trip to the sea, but I honestly forgot which came first (or last). Because it was relatively warm when we went to the sea, it makes sense that it probably occurred after winter, and I shall present it as such. Whatever the case, what is known is that after the big trip to the sea, I left Casa Doi.

PART THE FIFTEENTH

Whereas I have a Big Christmas Party & I Go to the Black Sea

Later, the days got darker and the air got colder. I would sit by the window and stare out the window down below to the trees that were losing colors and the people that talked less and walked faster. Everything got more and more silent, and less people came to see us. The days grew more boring, and we got into more fights. It was on this account that I remember a few things. Firstly, I lost my voice one day (probably from screaming too much), and I was scared that I was dying. It was the first time I realized how awful it was that no one could understand me. My voice was important to me because I could not sing, which was one thing I really enjoyed doing, and the fact that I couldn't be bossy, which was how I tried to maintain control. Both aspects were bad, and I was completely and utterly terrified of this. However, I regained my voice again the next few days, and I was much relieved.

The second thing was the recital. Now, I was known to sing, and sang quite good at that, so I was selected to do a recital of some sort in front of a large group of people. Personally, I refuse to recount the fact that I had to put on a bunny/rabbit costume on as part of this recital, but the matter is true-I had to wear a stupid costume of such likeness-and I was more worried about screwing up my lines than the costume I wore. At school, I had to sing for the parents and I felt quite proud to showcase my voice. My voice was very good: I don't remember it, but everyone said it was amazing, and I believe it because I sang so much and I loved to sing all the time about everything, which means I had a lot of practice. I was one that really enjoyed putting on performances because I took center stage. That being the case, we had to practice for such a recital in that room upstairs that I had mentioned before and that was often grueling. I had to study hard to memorize (and memorizing things was not something I was really good at) and I would get slapped the hell of out of if I failed to either comply or execute my lines correctly. The room was like our torture room, because we got scared of screwing up and getting hit, not knowing whether we had said our lines correctly or not. I'm not even sure that it really helped, because either way, I was still really nervous. I would break in a sweat, I would feel like a knot was growing in my throat, and I would get a little dizzy. It was really hard.

We also had to do something on television, and I recall how everything was so weird. There were big teddy bears that we orphans had to hug while we said something to the camera. It was quite ironic because there was a man in the background dressed in a jolly joker costume-and who looked the least interested to be there. In fact, he had a short temper and was smoking practically the whole time. I was utterly amazed how he transformed, though, when the lady at the camera would tell us that we start. Every time we started, he acted funny and like another person. But, when the lady told us we had to stop, then he went back to being quite angry and looking like he hated all of us kids in the studio. I found this quite fascinating. It was like being two people. At the time, I wasn't really aware that he was an actor and that we were probably doing a charity event of some sort. I found all this quite strange but fascinating. On Christmas Day, several of the girls even went on television and received presents from some popular television personalities, which was really cool. I thought it was amazing that I actually knew the girls on television. It was as if they were famous now, and I was living here in the orphanage with them.

That Christmas was really special. It was really special because I got presents for the first time (I don't recall what I got though-it certainly must not have lasted very long). It was also really special because we had a Christmas tree that lighted up and would sing songs with the lights. I found this really fascinating and really beautiful. The songs had that electronic sound to them, the songs that everyone knows, like "Jingle Bells", "Silent Night", and so forth. It was literally the most beautiful thing I had seen up to that time. There was just something special about Christmas when you are an orphan. This mysterious feeling of complete loneliness can be weirdly beautiful. It's as if you lack any existence and you are nothing, and that can be relieving. It makes you feel that you have no stress. It's a feeling that is hard to explain, because it is essentially innocence at play. When you are an orphan, you are completely helpless, and this helplessness is, in a way, a form of innocence. It's as if you can do no wrong because you are not accountable to anything. You depend so much on others that you are purely at the whim of external forces. As such, Christmas seems to have sparked this special feeling in me. Of course, I gave no thought to it any other time of the year. But Christmas always seems to bring this feeling about in me. I was, essentially, experiencing the same innocent feeling that the miserable match girl was feeling on that cold

Christmas Eve night. In this, I can completely relate with Han Anderson. He must have felt this way as a child, because he certainly portrayed it well in his stories.

Christmas Eve was the weirdest night I remember. It had snowed, and we walking that night looking at the snow while our caretaker was telling us stories about something which I don't recall. She answered our questions we had about Christmas and how special it was. I, as usual, was being obnoxious, and pissed off one of the caretakers. When we went back into Casa Doi, she left me outside as punishment. However, as I waited in the shivering cold for what seemed like hours on end, she must have forgotten me at the footsteps at the front of the orphanage. I saw the last light go out upstairs, and I knew that they were now smoking and talking amongst themselves. I tried yelling, but I was told to shut up, so it was clear to me that they still knew I was out there. I started crying, because I thought that they thought I was pathetic, and out of anger, I walked away from the orphanage. I started walking on the main road towards the main gate. The air was so still, and the sky was very clear. As I walked on the main circle, the lights stringed across the light pots were all lit, and they dangled. It was really beautiful and spectacular, and I looked at them for some time. They were so comforting and pretty, that I sat by the main lamppost and stared at them. I was really tired from crying and throwing at fit from earlier on. So, I fell asleep, by the lamppost in the middle of the main circle by the main gate, amongst the dangled Christmas lights. I remember that it was the weirdest nap I've ever had, though I couldn't recall it for the life of me.

I just know that when I woke up, I couldn't tell if I was dreaming or sleeping. I was just so cold that I was numb.

I was shaken awake by a guard at the front gate. He wrapped me in his coat, since I was extremely cold, and took me back to Casa Doi. One of the night caretakers took me upstairs and put me to bed. I don't recall what she said to the officer, because I was so tired, but she seemed slightly shocked. I fell fast asleep, and awoke the next morning as if nothing had happened. It was while we were walking to Christmas mass when I noticed the dangling lights and remembered the previous night. And I thought it strange, because the main circle looked nowhere near as magical and beautiful as it did in the night. But, so it was. Every child, I suppose, has his or her time in their lives when a situation occurs and it becomes magical for a reason they can't comprehend.

The staff got nicer, for some reason. There wasn't as much commotion as before. Days seemed very fast. We would spend our times clustered around the windows, watching the world below, cold and white, snow falling slowly and the stars shining dimly in the dark sky at night. It was really cold because, for some reason, our electricity didn't work so well. There were typical nights when we would have no light at all, and we had to use candles to light the orphanages while the caretakers huddled in their lounge room warming themselves in the little stove they had and drank hot drinks. All of us orphans were always cold and immobile. Everybody seemed dead. I felt that I, too, crawled in my tree, and awaited for the time for God to unleash his tears so that I could move again.

Well, spring did come. It came very fast. The cherry tree blossomed again, and I rushed to grab its cherries before anyone else did. I climbed the trees in our front yard and picked up all the berries I could find. We all started going barefoot again and wearing less clothing. The abuse went back to normal (which meant going back to being horrible again), and I remember that me and another person tried telling the boss lady about it, but she just laughed at us when we told her what we were going through. She told us that we had good imaginations and that we deserved to get beaten because we were bad kids. I thought it was rather ironic that we even talked to her because I suddenly realized that she was no better than the orphanage caretakers.

However, I was able to make an acquaintance with the boss lady more often because I was going through adoption. You can imagine my utter surprise when I saw her office. It was truly big. It was nice. She had a nice desk. Everything looked nice and tidy, and very professional. There were tons and tons of what looked like donated goods and toys in the closet in front of her desk. The boss lady, as was typical, was dressed in a nice suit. She had a computer, and her office, I swear, was nicer than the head chancellor of our school. It was weird seeing this kind of environment when the rest of the orphanage was in shatters and was literally being torn down by us orphans smashing our heads in the windows or walls, or being thrown against them, or simply because no one took good care of the place.

Anyhow, we would talk, especially about school and such, and then she would tell me I had some appointments with some very important people. Whereas, on those days, she would take me with her to these court meetings and the like. She spoke for me on almost all occasions. In fact, I don't recall one time I ever stepped into a court to speak on my behalf. One time, while the boss lady was getting something from her car, I saw many donated toys and goods in her car. It was then that I started realizing that she took all the donations, along with the caretakers. No wonder why we weren't getting anything. I remember telling the other orphans about it, and they really began to despise the boss lady quite a lot. When I told Jeppa and Roberto about it, they told me that they already knew and that they would get some of the donations, especially if it was candy. This made me realize that perhaps my adopted family had sent me more candy and presents and Roberto and Jeppa had probably eaten them. To me, it made perfect sense, because Roberto and Jeppa were actually chubby fellows, while everyone else was small and thin. They never were hungry (and were the only ones that I recall, except for the girls, to refuse food sometimes). Everything started clicking, and I remember being so angry about it that I swore I would kill them if I could. However, I wasn't known to really hold long grudges, so my feelings passed through and I got along with them again.

Once, when I was walking to the park with everyone, two men came up and asked out loud which person was named "Nicolae Viorel Burcea". There was a hesitation amongst everyone. Everyone started looking at me, because I was the only one whose name was Nicolae. However, I was very confused, because I never heard anyone use my first real name before, and I had never heard the word "Burcea" being associated with me. Even I was looking around asking others who was "Nicolae Burcea". However, someone spoke up, and told them that I was the person they were looking for, and they placed me in their car and we drove to a picture studio. It was my first time riding in a small car, and I felt extremely special because I felt really important. I recall marveling at the seat beat, and trying to push myself up to see over the window as we drove around the Arch. We went to get my picture taken, and all I remember of that place was that I was given a white shirt to wear and told to smile. I found it really hard to smile, just like Ms. Debbie had tried to do, so it was always forced. The only way I could smile was if the camera guy told me a funny joke. I remember he was really friendly and really funny, and I got my picture taken and I went back on the excursion that our group had gone on. The last I remember of that day was one of the caretakers making a comment to the men that a kid like me didn't deserve to be adopted to America, where everyone was rich. She seemed all snobby about it, and she seemed to puff on the cigarette she was smoking more than usual and she gave a look of total disgust at me. Her sharp eyes were empty, like the little girl that I saw when I met my adopted family.

Later, the air became warm and spring was definitely in the air. I think it was nearing summer, because it was actually getting hot. The next memory I have was when I saw the caretakers pack and we knew something was happening. Usually, the orphanage ladies wouldn't tell us if we were leaving, as often this caused a lot of commotion, but, when you have nothing better to do but sit in an orphanage and try not to get beaten the hell out of, then of course, you take notice of things like when caretakers pack. I went to bed that night, and the girl that slept next to me was moving her head from left to right over and over again. I thought this was interesting, and so I tried it until (later) it became a habit. It was soothing and it cancelled out all the noise, which was a problem in the orphanage.

The next day, we were rounded up. We were divided in groups and we walked all the way to the nearby train station. It was very thrilling because I had never ridden a train before, and it seemed like a huge mystery and awesome experience. We got on the train and were escorted to our booths in large numbers (my booth had like eight people). We were all stuffed, and it was the first time I noticed that our clothes were dirty compared to the other kids on the train. The train started rolling, and we looked out the windows, not budging, else we pissed off the caretakers (who had warned us previously that we would get a heavy beating if we failed to be "good", meaning complainant, of course). We smelled food from the other booths, but we didn't eat anything, as we hadn't brought anything for the trip.

It is quite difficult to describe how beautiful the countryside looked as the train sped East to the Black Sea. There were sunflower fields that stretched forever. Everything looked very natural and calm, quite unlike that of Bucharest, which was always busy and noisy. The scenery was exceptionally beautiful. There was dark green rolling hills and forests that seem to cover the landscape like patches on a quilt.

This was something I didn't recall ever seeing before, so it looked really pretty. I had thought that the landscape looked like the pictures in my Fairy Tale books at school.

However, all this fascination took only a hold of me for a brief moment. I fell asleep on the train and didn't wake up until we got to the beach

I awoke to a completely different city. The air smelled of water, and I could see far in the distant the sea. We were vacationing at the sea. For me, this was a glorious moment. Everything was so new and people were so happy. Everyone was smiling and laughing. The sky was so clear, and the water looked a really fantastic color of green and blue. And the air was absolutely perfect, even at night, where the breeze was as soft as a leaf falling slowly to the ground, swaying ever so lightly with the slightest touch of the wind.

We were all escorted into a hotel of some sort, where long white beds were prepared for us. Most of us were on good behavior, as we knew that if we acted good, we could do better and cooler things throughout our vacation here at the sea. I think all of us were in such awe at the sea and how beautiful everything was: the music was amazing, the food we were served was the best I'd ever have, the sand was great, and the sun was bright and welcoming. None of us were allowed in the water, so we sat on the beach, watching other people swim. We played beach soccer and ran around in the sand. I was very happy. Every few thousand meters or so, there would be lifeguard posts were loudspeakers were attached. Here, people would come and do karaoke at the beach, which blasted from the loudspeakers. People would gather around and cheer them on.

We took many walks, as this was common in all our vacations. We would walk for several kilometers a day. I saw many beautiful things that I don't remember now, but I know that they were beautiful. I was never upset or depressed on this trip. Up to that time, it was the happiest thing I'd ever done. At night, when the moon was out and it shone on the water, I would stare out from the clear windows and looked how beautiful and peaceful the sea was, lined up with boats and little lighted candles. It was truly very calming and it helped me fall asleep several times. It seems as if these quite times were the most mysterious for me, as if I suddenly grasped the meaning and purpose of life's biggest questions, only for them to slip away as if I had been dreaming and it became an understood part of me, but only in my subconscious. I would realize I was small and there was a big world. But such feelings quickly escaped me as I fell asleep and awoke the next morning to loud calls.

One night on this vacation of ours, one of the caretakers stated that whomever was the best that day would go on an outing with her at night. I was very interested, so I shut my mouth as I knew best to do sometimes, and was as brilliant of a child as I possibly could, with the hope that I would be selected. Well, my efforts came to be fruition because I was allowed to come, after I kept nagging them about it. Helga and I were the only two that were allowed to go. This was the first time I had realized that I was a favorite to some of the caretakers, for a reason I'm unable to comprehend, as I was a terrible child when I was an orphan and I gave many issues to anyone dealing with me.

Anyhow, we went out that night. I was truly amazed by everything I saw. At night, it seemed, everyone was alive and dancing, with loud music and lots and lots of food everywhere. For an orphan whose number one concern is usually food, this seemed like paradise. And it was. I saw fire everywhere, and the smell was absolutely fantastic. I heard a lot of music and people were dancing everywhere. The air was stanched everywhere with beer and whiskey, but people seemed to luxure in the realm of drinking alcohol. It was the first time I saw people partying, and it seemed exhilarating to me. Such things made me feel so much a part of the group that I felt I could blend in and nobody would notice my existence. Indeed, such a feeling was great, and I wanted to stay there forever.

However, all things are short, and the same can be said about our stay at the big party. I was grabbed by the hand and was dragged by the drinks, the fire that roasted meat that smelled the best I've ever smelled, the dancing people that seemed to be in ecstasy, and the music that seemed to consume the life out of the people whom danced to it. That being said, I was escorted to a stage where people were singing. Here, I saw people, young and old, sing songs about many things. I do not remember anything other than the song *"0 Portocala"*, which I have no idea what it means other than the fact that it had a very catchy tune and I heard that song earlier that day on the beach being sung by a pretty girl in a bikini by one of those big loudspeakers. That girl was singing the tune then, and she was wearing an all-white suit. I was wonder struck by all this, and the last I recalled was how two of the singers were kissing nearby me, and I thought that it was weird how music made people do strange things. It was beautiful, but at the same time it was uncomfortable.

I do not remember much more from that vacation, other than staying up late at night, cold (because we were given no blankets to sleep with), and staring out the window while listening to the soft sounds of the ocean waves crashing into the beach below us. For me, it was amazing being at the beach, and how wonderful it felt seeing the world, and people, and sand, and water, and everything else that comes with the beach. Today, I often wonder how I could look at such simple things and be so awed about them. Most of the times, I was behind walls of some sort, so such vastness and beauty would truly grasp my imagination, and it is amazing how ignorance can sometimes make the most obvious things be the most beautiful and incredible feelings ever experienced. If falling in love is one of the most beautiful things to experience, then one should put amazement and wonder as a close second.

I must add that this beach story ends here-that means that I have absolutely no idea what happened later. I do recall that after we came back, we were reassigned again, and we were placed on buses once more. We waited upstairs while the caretakers name called, and we went our separate ways in the buses that sped out accordingly to the orphanages. At the time, Casa Doi was the happiest place I had known up to that time, due to the fact that I did so many things that I really enjoyed. Looking back now, Casa Doi was one of my worst periods in my life, as the abuse was often unbearable, but, considering that I was often an optimistic child, full of life and curiosity, I could see that being able to do more things was indeed a good thing for me. Casa Doi was to be better than the next orphanage I would attend, but I had no clue. No one really expects terrible to go to worse. But such is the reality of life. I was about seven and a half when I moved to my next orphanage. I would have about a year left.

PART THE SIXTEEN

Whereas I Relocate to My Sixth and Last Orphanage
and I Start Thinking More

Our last orphanage was situated a little way from the city of Bucharest. It was more rural, with trees everywhere, chickens running about, and people wearing more rugged clothes. When we arrived at the orphanage, it was more than clear that the building had been a hospital of sorts. We were all escorted to one room, stuffed really, and had our names called one by one, according to the assigned rooms for each of us. I was chosen to be with the older kids, so I got the room in the very back of the orphanage.

Admittedly, this orphanage was better in the sense that there was an air conditioning system, beds we could sleep on with pillows and blankets, tables and chairs that we could sit in and eat, and carpets on the floor. It was just bigger. The orphanage was like a U-shaped building. There was a gate in the front, an old wooden abandoned building by the kitchen part, and a big open area that was enclosed by the whole orphanage. There was a second floor, where the laundry would get done and where there was a huge open space which no one used. The other side of the orphanage was completely abandoned. Nobody lived there, and everything smelled of dust and old papers. The basement of the orphanage was also abandoned, and looking down from the small barred windows, one could look back in time. Papers were still on the desks, scrambled about. The drawers were still heavily shut, and all the offices looked as if someone has just been ordered to leave and take nothing. It was like a snapshot of the past, secured in place only visited by the countless dust particles floating in the air every day. The whole place looked extremely creepy, and I have had so many nightmares just imagining the possible things that had occurred down in the basement before we orphans had come.

There really weren't any issues in the first few days adjusting to the new environment. Being so close to one another meant we could play more. We could eat all together, and so forth. However, such intense connections became more difficult to control when things got out of hand. For example, when the girls' dorm blew up with tantrums, hearing them made us riled up, and we started throwing tantrums. The caretakers became more physical in order to control us better. Also, we were older, which meant that we were getting stronger and more defiant.

Such behavior was held with great hatred. The abuse got ridiculously terrible. We would bleed from getting whipped so hard. We would blister and we cried like babies whenever we were going to get punished, which was every day. Getting hit was a routine, and it became a lifestyle for all of us. The anger built up in being hit so much exploded into huge fights, dealt with blows and physical attacks that were brutal and dangerous that left both the caretaker and the orphans hurt and wounded. What was amazing was the fact that these caretakers were women, huge and aggressive, boisterous, and cruel to an unbelievable level. If ever one could see ultimate hate, they would be its example. They were not only this way, but the girls were also just as bad. They broke into fights and were more aggressive than us boys. For this reason, and this reason alone, I came to be very skeptical of girls/women in general and viewed them as physical threats. This is why I had no problem punching girls as a child-most of them were bigger and more aggressive than me. The level of aggressive independence and mental retaliation would become quite weird as my adopted mother would show some of the qualities that some of the orphanage caretakers had, even though hers was for the better.

Perhaps more frightening to me was the fact that I had lost almost all my influence that I previously had in Casa Doi. This happened for two reasons; firstly, I was much younger. I was no longer equal to everyone's age range. Many of the new orphans were three to four years older than me, already in the teens or mid-teens. I could no longer compete physically with them, as they could easily beat me up in a few minutes. Secondly, some of the caretakers in the previous orphanage had come to the new orphanage, bringing with them their wisdom of my behavior and how to ensure that I could no longer become influential. They would purposely humiliate me and hurt me, as well as talk badly of me so that I became a troublemaker in reputation and an untrustworthy fellow at that. I became aware of their intentional downplay of who I was very clearly, for I wasn't stupid in that regard. I am well aware when people try to criminalize others because I was so good at doing this myself.

Such circumstances played hard on me, as for the first few months, this was a critical problem. I got beaten up more than ever before. Food was stolen from me every day. I was taunted and pranked upon until I became miserable and scared shittless. This environment had my mind racing to how to address the new situations. I could no longer be physically aggressive. That in itself was a huge problem. It therefore occurred to me that I had to lie more, be more effective at it and pursue it more. In order to not be caught up with the lie, I felt that I had to lie to everyone. That way, it caused confusion and nobody understood anything. Also, something that would become invaluable to me was making alliances so that bigger, stronger people could cover for me and so it could refocus and shift the problem to them. Meaning that I had to sweet talk others into trusting me. That was the hardest thing to do, but this was something that would become the most valuable asset in my life. Corresponding with others in the most diplomatic way possible became a trait of mine, as I had to make the other person feel as if I understood them so well that they would trust me. My personality would adapt to what they liked, and thus they would feel as if they could relate to me, thus they would end up trusting me because I was similar to them. This idea was revolutionary for me because it both implicated my safety and their loyalty. What became more important to me (and them) was my ability to extract personal information, and keep it secretive, sometimes only revealing it as a weapon in which to weaken someone's influence or ability to do something. I became extremely sneaky and cunning, and it is a trait that has been a part of me as I continued growing up. Now, such ideas are way ahead of my level of thinking for a seven-year-old. After all, if a child starts thinking this way, many people ought to get extremely worried. However, for me, I believe I thought these ideas subconsciencously, and just observed that they were highly effective. I mean, it doesn't take much brains to figure out how people act in situations. Also, it's not like I had a choice. I had to figure something out or else it was going to end extremely bad for me.

Such ideas brought me to think more. When I realized how talking to people made me more influential, it really did occur to me to think more. For the first time, I was able to develop short ideas, and to contemplate the idea of what I did ended up getting me. Of course, my perception was short sighted. I used my understanding of previous encounters to determine new encounters. Therefore, sometimes, I would get caught up in my own scheme and be acknowledged as a weasel. However, this only happened when people actually took care to notice me and help me out. Typically, my actions usually worked and it got me a benefit somehow. Within half a year, I became a favorite to many of the caretakers for my charming behavior and (at the same time) my trouble-like behavior. I was still highly defiant and aggressive-that never really left me-but I was more calculating. Needless to say, I became more like Ionut and Jeppa than I'd ever realized.

This new orphanage did open up a lot of new things to me. Because the others were older and knew more, I learned more about drugs and sex than anywhere else. Indeed, I still don't recall ever being sexually abused, but it seems highly possible due to the fact that I still have faint recollections of sexual exposure. Not enough to make the reality sustainable, but ideally enough for it to be highly plausible.

This orphanage was brutal from the start to its finish. It was cold all the time, it was scary because it was a hospital falling apart, and it was always dark because every light seemed to be out. The air was filled with dust, and the place was surrounded by high concrete and brick. Outside the on the side of the orphanage was a big concrete wall where, over it, a family of dark-skinned people like me lived. Inside the courtyard, the grounds were concrete, broken into millions of cracks and weeds growing everywhere. The place looked haunted, and it seems none of us really liked the place anyway.

Anyhow, we got a new boss-lady, as was typical. She was meaner than the last, and fatter. She had her office right by a very nice caretaker lounge, which I've only been in once, and it looked very nice, with seats and a television and a fridge and drinks. The new caretakers were tougher and meaner. The new orphans were much older. Ionut, Jeppa, Roberto, and Helga all came with me to the orphanage. The dorm I was in had about fifteen or so beds, with a television, some chairs and tables, several closets, a clock, white walls, a carpet, and two big windows and two doors. When we were not outside, we were in our dorms, either watching boring television or getting punished. Also, when we went to eat, we all walked to the big cafeteria in a line, where everything was cold and the food was alright. One other aspect about this orphanage was that we all got sick more times than we could count, and one person in our dorm later died from "choking from an apple core", although more likely than not, he died because he was extremely sick, like all of us.

PART THE SEVENTEENTH

Whereas I go back to School, Learn to Read and Write, and Accept no Adoption

Shortly after the move, I was placed back into school. I went with three girls, Helga included. The school was much bigger than my previous one. Unlike the last one, this one was much farther away and by a lot of trees. Not only this, though, but it wasn't as modern. It had a more traditional feel to it, with wooden tables and floors. We didn't have to have a dress code, like the other school, and there were more students. My classroom was upstairs on the second floor. Considerably, this was my first "normal" Romanian school, as I did tests and had a normal day of exercises, such as social studies and mathematics.

I could not afford to buy my own book, thus, the teacher let me have hers. Unlike the previous teacher, she was nicer and more willingly to help me out. Every day, we sat down and went over words and how to spell well. I learned very quickly, as I actually enjoyed school very much. Being able to play with the students was also very enjoyable for me. Not only this, but we did a lot of fun activities together. I was still placed in the back of the class, but only when I had bad behavior. Usually, I sat with a girl near the front of the class. I don't remember too much about the girl other than the fact that she seemingly had a lot of food with her all the time, and that I tried to steal her food almost every day, to which I was somewhat successful. I must add that she usually didn't notice that I stold her food, which goes to show how much she brought every day.

Whenever I went back to the orphanage, I would have to sit down and finish my assignments. For me, this was terrible, because I would get hit every time I made a mistake. Luckily, though, some of the caretakers were adamant about me learning, and they did take some time out of their lives to teach me numbers and how to spell and read. Indeed, I learned fast, so as to not get whopped, and therefore memorized all I could. There was one particular cruel caretaker who would supervise me in my reading and writing assignments, and this was quite awful for she would literally breathe down my neck and slap me when I least expected it, especially if I stumbled on the words.

When we walked to school, which was every day, a caretaker would take us. We would get out around noon or so, and she would be there to take us back. Sometimes, she would be extremely nice and let us go play at the playgrounds before we came back to the orphanage. It was around one of times when I went on a seesaw and accidentally slipped my finger through the bend and cut my finger severely bad. While Helga and the other girl freaked out, the caretaker could care less, so my finger was extremely injured for years to come, as I came to have a habit of sucking at it and biting it whenever I got nervous. However, the very fact of knowing that people didn't care for me being hurt or not really made me realize that there really was no one in the world who did anything nice for me with a good intention. Nice people were not nice. They just seemed nice because they liked and did some things that I liked and did. It made sense to me because the reason the orphanage caretaker let us go to the playground was because she didn't like the orphanage any better than we did, so she tried to avoid the place as much as possible.

School had a huge impact on me. Firstly, the reason I was going was because I was getting adopted. That in itself was reassuring. Secondly, it made me feel that I was getting better and better than the orphans because I was one of the very few students who could attend, and I was getting smarter than them. It became a sport for me to spout facts and to work hard to memorize them from school every day. Finally, school helped me see a world beyond that of the orphanage. I learned (for the first time), that the whole world wasn't just Romania, and that there were other countries. I first heard of the United States of America over an announcement of an attack on two big towers in a big city. I saw, on TV, a man who happened to be the country's President. I saw our President talk of a war in another country. Of course, I didn't come to understand until later that the news was about September 11, 2001. And I would come to know that the President was George W. Bush and that our President was speaking about going to war in the Middle East with the U.S. over terrorism.

That being said, school was enlightening to me, because deep within, it was another world. I became very excited to know so many things and do everything. I was curious about everything, and I would go around trying to analyze everything. It secretly made me self-aware that I did not know much about what I knew. Therefore, I tried to know more. For some reason, I had more desire to learn than anyone else in my orphanage, including the girls that went with me. I felt destined to be better. Or maybe I just really wanted to be better. Either way, I had a strong desire to be successful.

It was around this time when I received some new donations by my host family. Inside were some toys, candies, and a picture book. The caretakers took a lot of interest in the picture book, which showed my family's house, backyard, and their children. They would go through and mumble roughly to themselves. The front picture, which was a photo of the house in United States, would make them really angry. For me, I wasn't really well aware why. Today, I'm aware that they were extremely envious that the house my adopted family owned was so huge and nice looking. Indeed, it was like being taunted, to know that a small kid who was nobody to them, was going to live in this nice house, which looked like a mansion. This kid who was a troublemaker, who didn't work hard for anything, or struggled hard to make money and take care of children of his own. This kid who was magically being dumped into a princely life. To them, it certainly didn't seem fair. They were well aware that I was extremely blessed, but they despised me for it. I would get made fun of and taunted over it. Sometimes, they would make my punishments worse because I was "leaving anyway". It was clear that I was becoming a symbol of harsh reality to them.

While this was the case for the caretakers, this wasn't the case for the other orphans. I became interesting to them. They begged me to take them with me, and I would promise them that I would, even though I had been to enough court sessions to know that the idea was completely absurd. I was hearing that the adoption was taking a really long time. I wasn't really aware why. I would get my hopes up, as the people I would go with would tell me "soon", but months would pass and they would hear no more. Pretty soon, I gave up complete hope. I was sincerely sure that the process had stopped, like for the ones in the other dorms, who were not leaving after having been told that they were. Even Helga, who was going to be adopted by American parents, didn't leave. Her family gave her some American money, which she gave to me. So, here I was, reading the Latin words on the coins, and then slowly pronouncing the U-N-I-T-E-D S-T-A-T-E-S O-F A-M-E-R-I-C-A on the penny, only to think I would never go there. It made me mad in a way, but I didn't have a close enough connection with my adopted family to be angry at them-I simply didn't know who they were. So, I would scroll through my picture book and wonder who everybody was and what the English words meant. I remember noticing the girl I had met earlier and seeing her again in the pictures. She no longer had the hollow eyes anymore (or as much). But she had a weird smile. All the others just looked really unfamiliar to me. And when the caretakers caught me looking at the picture book, they would make rude comments, and just remind me that nobody wanted me, that's why I hadn't left yet. And the other orphans would look at me as if I had let them down, and that I had lied to them. Although I didn't really care too much about the other kids, I really only cared about how the others perceived me. I was very sensitive to whether my peers liked me or not.

The boss-lady would tell me that I was like the pauper who became the prince. I had no idea that she was referring to the book by Mark Twain. I actually took that literally, that I was going to become a prince. Such thoughts were great to me, but the fact that I hadn't left made me feel that the caretakers were right-I wasn't leaving. By the time six months came around, I was almost sure I wasn't leaving ever. That it was all a joke. Helga and I would talk about it. However, unlike me, she was sure she was leaving, whereas I had just given up on it. I wouldn't hear about my case again.

PART THE EIGHTEENTH

Whereas I Experience the Essence of My Country
While on a Vacation

Some time passed before we were off to another expedition, this time to the Mountains. The vacation is, and was, the most memorable thing I had ever done in my life. The reason was that it was the only time I went sightseeing and I did not get hurt in any way. I enjoyed life and could be a kid wherever I was. The moment is also special because it was the first time when I really could relate to the idea of my country's identity as Romania.

Unlike last time, the orphanage had some of us divided. That meant that each dorm went on a separate outing of their own. My dorm was headed for the mountains while others went elsewhere. Actually, this was great because we didn't have to have so many people come along with us. Not only that, but because of the split, the caretakers could split up to destinations they wanted to go. What was really brilliant was the fact that our group actually got the best caretakers in the orphanage. They weren't the best, mind you, they were just the ones that gave no shit what we did, which is equivalent enough to say that they were the best because we could do what we wanted. They were still mean, but that was only when you got on their nerves. If none of us did piss them off, then we could literally do what we wanted.

So, off we went, on the bus, rolling up and down through the hills, watching expanses of trees appear before us. We caught sight of villages dotted throughout the land, distanced sporadically. The roads got thinner, and we went much higher, where we had to wind on the roads. The scenery was absolutely amazing. What was also interesting was that we orphans were so captivated by this new change of scenery (from that of the city) that we were all silent and in awe. It was as if we went from a place compacted by people to that of a place that no one ever used. The trees seemed ancient. The hills seemed ancient. Even the sky had a darker color to it, as if it had worn itself for millions of years and had gotten old. For some reason, the scenery reminded me completely of the old books that I read at the library. Even though the book's smell wasn't present, the feeling of it certainly was. Romania is, after all, a really beautiful country. Its scenery is like magic and mystery. The forests seem to engulf everything, holding centuries old secrets that no one knew. It's hard not to feel attached to this land. The country has fought for over 2,000 years to maintain this land, so it's certainly special to us. The feeling that one has for this land is quite unexplainable. It was this feeling I got as we drove down the winding roads far up into the mountains.

After driving all day, we reached a hotel on top of a big cliff. The hotel was made of wood, and it stood three or four stories high. It had spirals and looked very fine. The woodwork on it looked absolutely phenomenal. The hotel had a courtyard in the front, where there were loudspeakers and a bar that served soda and drinks. Here we sat down and were given food as we were assigned rooms. I can't express how amazed I was by the food, how good it tasted. The bread was phenomenal, the meat was the best I'd ever eaten, and the drinks, whatever it was (I think it may have been an alcoholic beverage) was warm and very filling. For the first time in my life, I was full. Fuller than the parties where they hung cookies on playground areas. Fuller than that party where I was stuffed with watermelon. I was full and content. So we just sat there, while we watched the sun set in the rolling hills below. It was such a pretty view, and I remember making the remark that we should run and catch the sun the next day. It looked like a fantasy picture. All it needed was a castle, but I needn't worry. Romania has plenty of those all over the country. I certainly felt that the hotel was one anyway, since the whole place looked and smelled ancient and incredibly traditional.

We went to our assigned rooms, which were remarkably nice. Each room held two beds. Not only this, but it also had a nice-looking iron fireplace where you could warm the room and heat up your coffee/tea. It looked so tidy in the room that I felt that I was living in a king's palace. The whole hotel smelled of wood and food and it overlooked atop all the hills and mountains beyond. In many ways, the decorations of the hotel made it look as if I was living in a mansion. It was incredible. We went on the balcony at night and looked at the view for a few minutes when the loudspeakers down below started playing traditional music and the latest pop songs. It gave a very nostalgic feeling to it. We later went to sleep and I remember falling asleep feeling very relaxed.

The next day, we were awakened rather early, where we were fed a quick breakfast, which was amazing, I might add, and then we headed out for the hike in the hills and forests. We all felt that we were all leaving the hotel (which we imagined as a castle) for down below to fight monsters or something. This was how all day went. We would pick up sticks and have sword fights, and pretended that we were marching into a great battle. We would point to the numerous sheep and cows that we would pass by and act as if they were the enemy. However, it is amazing how huge they were compared to us, and none of us dared touch them. We met shepherds. We went into parts of forests, where the trees loomed high and dangerously. We walked to a nearby village where we filled our liter bottles with ground water and got food to eat.

The villages were simpler, made of wood and stone. The churches looked much smaller than the ones in the city, and the villagers wore more traditional clothing. There were also tons of chickens running everywhere. The air was clearer, too. Everyone seemed much nicer.

The day was very peaceful. We didn't encounter a lot of people while we hiked. We were left to ourselves and the huge expanse of land that seemed to only be inhabited by wolves and bears and horses, all of which we saw. On a particular hill that we sat for rest, we made a game of who could catch a rabbit first. Some of us did, but I was unsuccessful because of their speed. They always seemed to ditch us at the last moment by jumping into the trees. The caretakers left us primarily alone, so we just followed along, like sheep. We saw much of nature, too much to detail everything. It's just important to say that everything was extremely beautiful.

The next few days were exactly like this. It was very peaceful, and I remember having a lot of fun. I remember the music, and how I suddenly noticed that I really liked it (the tigani-styled ones). We went to several restaurants that were amazing. The tables were made of wood, and had a very mountainous smell to them. The food was perfect every day. Back at the hotel, the bartender down below in the courtyard came to like me somewhat, and he let me try small amounts of all the beverages in his outdoor bar. A majority of it was beer, vodka, and whiskey, however, I stuck to the idea that they all tasted terrible (even though the smell was much nicer) and that I would just stick with Coca-Cola, because I came to really like the drink with all its flavor and its tinkling in my mouth, especially when we were eating.

Late at night, we would sit around the round wooden tables in the courtyard and talk about random things. When we got bored, we got up on the tables and danced to the music on the loudspeakers while we sang the sounds. We would play games, and the winner would have his glass filled up with a drink from the loser's glass. As we could only get three drinks a day, this made things very competitive. However, for some reason, everyone was very obedient and complaint. None of us had any fits or disturbances on this trip, and I ponder whether it was because we were happy or because the caretakers were not so cruel and mean then. In fact, they seemed to be as carefree and relaxed as we all were. Not only this, but they would sit around in one of the restaurants in the hotel, in which, by the corner, a fire was ablaze and people sat around it drinking and talking amongst themselves, while we gathered around the oldest caretaker and listened to her tell us folk tales and stories. Many of the stories, I found out, were Russian. Some, like Stan Bolovan and Vasilica the Brave, are definitely Romanian. Whatever the case, the dark woods below, the fire that was bright and warm, the aroma of food everywhere, and a good tale about a prince or warrior going out and fighting made any night perfect. And what was unique was that the caretaker, whatever her name was, was very good at storytelling. In fact, most Romanians I know are good storytellers, but she had a unique way of telling the stories. Romanian folktales, if said correctly, are sarcastically witty and funny. This lady would always start off her storytelling with a phrase like "Long time ago, something very special occurred. It must have been special, else, we wouldn't hear about it today." And she made the stories come alive, because she was really good about making expressions, pausing at perfect timing, and then changing her voice to match her character. She was so amazing that, ironically, I only know her as being a super religious lady and the only one that I would ask any question to, because, unlike the other caretakers, she was not cruel and she was much older, and she was actually intelligent and educated.

We spent about a week or two at the hotel. While there, we visited many castles and fortresses and many, many churches. We saw a huge amount of land, as we were driven to many locations. We climbed a mountain where a religious site was, where I recall looking down at the farmland, forests, and hills below feeling like a god. We went into many towns and villages. We met many merchants along the way. I was amazed how nice people were to us. They gave us a lot of food and were extremely hospitable. Every time we entered a church or a holy place, people went exceptionally out of their way to help us out or make us comfortable. Merchants let us touch their goods, and even let us try their merchandise. Once, while we were in a town, we met a man who was selling boomerangs. He showed us how to use them, and then let us use them. Then, he simply gave them to us! And this is amazing because we were well aware that he handcrafted these things by himself.

In museums, we were given free tours. While we walked on the streets, women would give us food and drink. Once, we met a man who went completely out of his way to drive into town and buy us ice cream. This atmosphere was so different from the city that it completely took me by surprise. It made me feel really special. Not only this, but it was around this time when I started seeing foreigners. It was explained to me by guides and priests that many people came to Romania to look around and enjoy the scenery. It had never occurred to me that people came to visit Romania just to see what it was like. But, now that I saw them and realized that they really liked what they were seeing, it made me feel really happy that Romania was so beautiful that people wanted to come and see it. I felt a small tingling inside, and I somehow felt very proud to be a Romanian. I thought that, surely, no country could be as beautiful as Romania and it felt good that I somehow owned something that other people didn't have, that I was part of a people who were part of Romania. Of course, I never thought any more than this, as these complex thoughts are for more mature thinkers, and at the time, I just realized a distinction that Romania was not the world, people wanted to come to Romania because it was special, and I was a person that lived in a place that was not all the world, making me special as well.

It was then when I realized that the colors red, yellow, and blue that I was seeing on all the museums stood for

Romania, and that the song I stood up and sang every morning for class was the country's song. Now, the words somehow made more sense, especially when I went to the museums and physically saw pictures and artifacts about the battles Romania had fought to be free and be independent. My history information that I learned in class clicked with me. I suddenly understood a new way of thinking about Romanian history. I learned so much on the trip, like how, sometimes, workers died while building the roads, so they just buried them into the mountains with their names inscribed on the outside. All this made me think and make me have nightmares of being killed in battles by those artifacts and the mountains and hot tar and the like.

The whole trip was amazing, and I was very upset to leave the hotel, which I had gotten used to. I was sad to leave the food, and the mountains and hills, and lonely woods and sheep and cows and castles that rose in the air and churches that smelled of strong incense and people that were so nice to me. But it was very special- else, I wouldn't feel it would still be special today.

PART THE NINETEENTH

Whereas I Encounter a Worse Situation
Back at the Orphanage

I came back to the city, and the conditions back at the orphanage slowly became worse than when I left. This may have to do with the fact that newer orphans were coming. They were much older, and they were now living upstairs. The situations upstairs must have been absolutely terrible because we heard a ton of commotion. Truly, it must have been horrible. Luckily for the caretakers (and not so much for us orphans), at sixteen we were dumped on the streets. This is when we aged out of the system. I have heard other orphans say the age was eighteen, but honestly, I have always believed it was sixteen. However, I got this information from the other orphans, so it easily could be wrong. Almost all of us would age out, and most would later join gangs or go underground.

The abuse became quite unbearable at times. The older orphans would beat the living shit out of me, and what was more surprising to me, was that the older girls picked on us kids all the time. We would get slapped and hit. The girls were actually at times worse than the caretakers, having no problem catching us and humiliating us for fun. I remembered how ugly they were, and I questioned my idea why I desired to have a pretty girl from my previous school for myself. I truly hated life, and I felt that every day was a struggle not to get beaten and have my food stolen from me. Everyone around me seemed wicked.

At school, I started messing up. I ran out of ink in my fountain pen all the time (because I made so many mistakes that I had to revise so many things) and I would walk back and get beaten severely bad. I would be so used to people beating me up that when I went to bed, I curled up to a corner, and watched from a peep hole from the blanket. That way, I was always aware who might be coming to beat me up. I started developing a strategy of running away from practically everything. I became more defiant, and way more aggressive. Sometimes, I would punch and kick and run away. Running away was really effective because I had a lot of energy and the caretakers and the older orphans didn't want to run after me.

I became really antsy about everything. It was terrible. I was mad all the time. I developed a much stronger bond with all the members in my dorm, as sometimes they were the only ones in the orphanage who could defend me. It became a thing of "us versus them" mentality. The corruptness and number of orphans just made it impractical for anyone to have control, which made the whole place unstable. There would be nights when the old caretaker would lock our dorm, so that nobody could come in, as the whole orphanage was in hell for that night. Somehow, a kid got pissed above and threw a huge fight with another kid. His friends probably joined in and a huge confrontation took place. Most likely, the guys were punching the crap out of each other, the girls were pulling hair and repeatedly yelling, and the caretakers locked themselves in the lounge and let the orphans go at it. In all reality, there was little they could do. They simply were not strong enough to hold off the others. The older orphans were too strong and too violent. The caretakers were women, older ones at that, and whereas they could beat the living shit out of an eight-year-old, they couldn't do that with kids as old as fourteen or fifteen.

So, the orphanage was in complete chaos all the time. All of us younger ones were getting beaten up by both caretakers whose patience was worn thin, and by the older orphans who were almost sixteen, and who were probably scared shitless knowing that they would be kicked out in less than a year. In that time, they just became so physically violent that their outbursts extended beyond themselves to us younger orphans and the caretakers who made their lives as miserable as they made ours. So, we would huddle in our dorm as we listened to classical music on the television or late-night news. And we would listen to the commotion and I would feel sorry for that sore loser who was truly getting beaten the hell out of and whose flowing blood would stain the floor for years to come.

I think that this is really the essence of an orphanage. Absolute chaos, each kid fending for themselves. Older kids beating up younger ones. Younger ones getting beaten up so bad that many would be physically scarred. The older ones had become monsters, relieved of all remorse and compassion. Everyone was living for themselves. Time was spent idling away, sporting about, and getting into fights to maintain dominance. It was the most primitive of all environments. Life really can't get much worse, especially with little to no order. It's literally the worst nightmare, like a hunger game, or rather, more like a purge. I'm not really sure how to describe it, because it's just not a normal environment. It's anarchy, where everything goes. Such was the life of a Romanian orphanage.

For me, I could no longer be that honorable Roman gladiator I so loved and imagined myself to be. I couldn't fight anyone. I was weaker and I knew it, and this was an embarrassment for me. I developed a completely new concept of myself. I saw myself as a Roman Caesar. I would wear a red blanket around my neck and boss everyone around. I'm not sure where this crazy concept came to me that I was a prince or Roman emperor, but I took a great fancy to it and many people would go around and call me all sorts of nicknames, such as the "little prince", "Caesar", and some other mythological heroes who showed exceptional arrogance and got killed. It is indeed a trait of a Romanian to spout out some tale or analogy to teach and rebuke one for doing something they consider unfavorable and then turn around and do it themselves. Such was the case for the caretakers and older kids, but they too displayed every fault I had. My visible arrogance was really quite annoying and disturbing to most, especially to the extremes I took to remind everyone of my fascinations, even when I welcomed the insults and took pride in them. Turing bowls upside down and wearing them as crowns was really quite ridiculous, but it seems one thing I hadn't lost as a child (and as an adult) was my incredible imagination for the grandeur.

PART THE TWENTIETH

Whereas I Have My First Birthday and Develop Some Characteristics

So, one particularly miserable day, our orphanage doctor, Ms. Alexandra, took me, Roberto, Ionut, and another kid whose name is Fernando for a birthday of sorts, at McDonalds. Roberto wanted a flashlight, as was usual, and I wanted Coca-Cola. Fernando didn't know what he wanted, as he was actually not mentally capable of putting words together to say exactly what we wanted. However, we had lived with him for a long enough time to understand him completely, and it was clear that all he wanted to do was just go play on the playground at McDonalds. So we did, and Dr. Alexandra took a photo or two of us doing that. It was really a good time. It was while I was at McDonalds that Dr. Alexandra told me that I was eight years old, and that my birthday was in December, on St. Nicolae's Day. For me, this was a real shock. I didn't know I had a birthday. I didn't know how old I was, and I certainly didn't know anything more about my life other than that my name was Nicu and that my favorite color was red and my favorite thing I liked to eat was green beans and pork. I remember having a conversation with Dr. Alexandra about who my mother was, but I was answered with a lot of "I don't knows" more than any solid answer.

Other than this, it was around this time when I started thinking of right and wrong. I would start thinking a lot about being good or bad, and that, partially, was the result of an old caretaker we had. She happened to be our permanent caretaker for our dorm, as we were the youngest and she was the oldest, and she apparently did not get along with the girls. So, she was with us a majority of the time. To me personally, this was important because she was there for practically everything. She had, somehow, a unique way of making us all calm (I think it was because of the stories), and her personality was not aggressive. We felt very calm around her, even when we were defiant.

She helped me with my homework, she let us play whenever she could, sometimes she brought in homemade food, and, most importantly, at night, she would tell us things about being good or bad. Almost all her stories had a Christian twist to them, so she would tell us the story and then we would talk about it. It was a time where we could ask her questions that made us think about what the story meant. It was clear that she must have been a teacher beforehand, because she was good at engaging us in conversation. Most of all, she was good at influencing how we acted. Whenever she caught me doing something, I would feel bad about it. Today, I'm not sure if that is because I didn't want to disappoint her or because I truly believed what I did was bad.

I certainly was aware that I should not do bad things because God would punish me. I developed an idea that perhaps if I did many good things, it would cancel out all the bad things I did. Therefore, I became more giving. I enjoyed making people smile, so I gave them things whenever I could, especially the orphans who were younger than me, which wasn't any considering that I was one of the youngest there. Whatever the case, I tried to be nicer and better. Dr. Alexandra used to describe me as very intelligent, and I was very happy to have this quality. She would tell me that I was very bright and had a skill for being a leader. This was good news to me because I didn't want to feel like I was nobody. In life, I wanted to be important, I wanted to help people who were not lucky like me (meaning those that didn't have any food), and I wanted to be big and strong. Nonetheless, the one thing I came to really value above all else was my intelligence and curiosity to learn. Many people used to remark this about me, and I felt that this quality really made me unique in the bunch of orphans around me.

I had somehow become much more different than in the last orphanage I was at. I was always in conflict with myself. Sometimes, I would try to be different and be nicer, but I always ended up being much worse. I would take a real delight in instigating people and making them really mad. I became really power-hungry. Any chance I had in forcefully exerting my leadership was readily used. My arrogance was really flaring up. I remember having a sense of feeling that I was born special. I would go about in the orphanage acting like I was far superior to everyone, creating nicknames for myself wherever I was. I would become loud and demanding whenever I had the chance. Everything I did I seemed to believe I was the best at. If there was a competition, I would tell everyone I was the winner. If it was singing, I would say I was the best. If it was racing, I would race and push everyone out of the way to win. I would do this in everything. I tried to be the best at everything. In fact, I would purposely go around looking for ways to compete to prove how much better I was than everyone else.

However, I also became aware of my bad feelings. Most of these feelings came to be had from my time in school.

There, I would see a world I could not participate in. I heard and saw kids have normal lives that I would never participate in. I think it was strange for me to see parents pick the students up, and think it weird that kids wanted to listen to their parents. However, I saw that these parents bought these kids everything. Everything I saw in school books that I wanted, like toys or food, the kids would bring them in to show the class, and I would wallow in envy, wondering how I could not have these things. I think school was a real killer for me, because I could not compete with the other kids. These simply knew how to read and write better than me. They knew more things than I did. The only thing that I could do better than them was sports, but this was not really important in school. I can say that I never really enjoyed school as a child in Romania.

Of course, when I went to school, I would broodily look at all the other kids and wonder why I too wasn't like them. They had plenty of school supplies, whereas I had to contend to myself and whatever little I could have. There was no appreciation towards me and my study. I was sent to the back of the class for my obnoxious behavior, and this only furthered my isolation and disregard for the classroom. Perhaps the most dismantling thing was the teacher, who was young and very vibrant. She was very polite and nice, and I would envy the affection she had for the other kids. All of them except me.

Like most Romanian women, she was very respectable. She dressed well and she was careful to be professional and clean. As such, though, at times, she would wear what is fashionable but rather disrupting to the boyish eyes in a boring atmosphere such as the classroom. Perhaps I wasn't the only one who noticed, but I couldn't surely have been the only boy in the class to notice the almost transparent blouses she worse sometimes when teaching. I used to stare quite diligently, out of notice of course, at her naked torso through the blouse, noticing her firmly suited breasts and nibs, the first I ever recall seeing in my life at that point. The teacher wasn't awful looking, and me being quite rebellious towards any authority rather dimmed my liking her, but she seemed perfect enough for my prepubescent likings, and such view made me ponder on such a new feeling that burst in my body that was new to me and quite mysterious.

These vivid memories and recollections had a reminisant charm to them that I have never captured again. They seemed to have instilled a nature I wasn't able to capture then nor now. I can only say that I was both in awe of this view and utterly repulsed by it. I wasn't sure what I was feeling, but I was certain that my envy for her affection towards the others made me have mixed feelings. It was as if they could share in that delightful gracefulness that the teacher was able to bestow in the most polite and compassionate way. However, when she had to address me, she seemed uncertain-unsure, rather-of what to say to me. It was as if she became tense and restrained, and I would sense a superficiality formulate. And such formalities only seemed to fuel my bitter feelings and almost guilty uncomfortableness to which I had when I knew something about myself to which I could not bring to consciously realize.

Perhaps I subconsciously knew it. I knew that I lacked any innocence, that I was in a deprived state of being, lacking the essential desire I wanted, which was to be wanted. By somebody that I wanted to want me. Everything I wanted consisted in such purity, but I would feel as if I stepped in a foreign atmosphere. I saw this teacher as such a good person, whose calm and compassionate eyes and smiles, whose very presence attracted me and repulsed me at the same time. Seeing her perfect bare body under thinly veiled blouses seemed to stir in me a feeling of awe, as if she somehow was more perfect, and yet, a repulse which seemed to make me angry, because, perhaps, I felt that what I wanted I could only get by taking. Nobody would ever give it to me. When people gave me something I wanted, it seemed as if another force gave these things to me, such as pity or moral obligations. Nobody ever knelt before me and stared deep in my eyes, and had ever given me anything just because of me. There was no hug, or smile, or loving moment that I can remember. And that aspired me to really hate and distrust everyone. I became hawkish and bossy. My eyes would look down in such rebellion that one would have suspected I was a fallen angel too embarrassed and mad to stare at the very sliver of heaven's golden rays. What was I then but something almost evil, wishing well on no one and scheming plots with manipulating twists on how to embarrass and demean people. It was like I was always going around trying to undermine others and their goodness. These are the complications of a deep-rooted mind to which I was most accustomed to as this period in my life. I seemed to be conflicted with myself, but these were only brief thoughts that would pass in the dull days of school.

PART THE TWENTY–FIRST

Whereas My Stay in Romania Comes to an Abrupt End

All things being, time passed through and winter went. I attended more celebrations that Dr. Alexandra put on for us. One happened to be a Christmas party, whereas some of us orphans came and had a big meal with stupid umbrellas in our drinks and lots of toys for us to play with. There was a fish tank filled with all weird types of fish and this was rather fascinating to me. In the back of the room were many presents, and I recall that the whole party very superficial. I believe it was meant for us children who were about to get adopted. When spring came, we went out to more parks, and one time, the old caretaker took us for a visit back to Casa Doi in the city. The orphanage was now occupied with many babies- it was no longer for us older kids. Looking around the building that used to house us lads only a year ago filled with cribs upon cribs of babies had a weird feeling to it. It was hard for me to make anything out of this scene because it rather stunned me. The only memory that sticks with me is the cries of the babies. The crying. There was always crying. Orphanages and crying. All one and the same.

By the time summer came around, I was relatively fluent in reacting and writing Romanian. I learned a lot of history, and I had done extremely well on mathematics; above, in fact, than the other students in my class. School had let out, and now we were off, and all of us orphans went back to the gardens in Bucharest. We traveled the city and saw many buildings. I witnessed several musicals and plays. The days seemed to go very fast. A lot of our caretakers were retiring or getting replaced by newer ones, so we were getting younger caretakers who seemed nicer. The younger ones seemed much more educated. They dressed very well, and even lectured us on many topics. They would take us out on outings and explain to us what to do at a stop sign, or how to use the subway system, and how to be safe on the streets. A new nurse had come to the orphanage, and she took much delight in taking me, Helga, and Fernando, who apparently were her favorite, out for outings, where we picked berries and went to stores and look around. In our dorm, the cruelest caretaker would take me along with her to the outdoor market. Although she was exceptionally mean, she did seem to be a different kind of person to me when we were both alone. She would tell me what the names of the fruits were and she had me socialize with the merchants, some who knew her pretty well. It was then when I noticed that I was rather shy. It was the kind of environment I wasn't used to. So, I just smiled and stayed close to the caretaker.

I must take a moment to describe this particular caretaker. I do not really remember her very well, at least her features, but I do recall that she was quite short. She had a very strong personality, and she was viscous. Of course, this wasn't all the time. After all, no one is cruel all the time. However, she was quite cruel whenever she got mad, which was quite often. Her eyes would light up, and the whip would come out, and all of us orphans would buckle and run for our lives, quite literally. This lady knew how to provoke fear, and she certainly had an air of terror about her. However, her attitude really defied me, for anytime I would get a beating by her, I would burn with rage and attack her, causing her to leash out on me with rapid whippings and fists to my face. The more she beat me, the madder I would become, and the madder I became, the more I attacked her, and the more this would happen, the more I would get beat. It was a neverending cycle. I wouldn't be afraid of her, but I showed complete hatred for her, and she would smile her wicked smile as if she was pleased I hated her. I believed she was pure evil, and would put my life on it. Her presence brought all the orphans to obey her, and this power was really impressive. I would defy her nonetheless, and I then would get the brunt of her attacks because I was the only one in the orphanage who really would not listen to her, ever.

In the orphanage, I became more disobedient. My arrogance flared up, and I became extremely bossy and daring. I would take pride in defying the caretakers and boldly stepping up to receive my punishment. Anytime I got hit, I would act like it did not bother me. In fact, when I got beaten, all the others would head for the beds and observe while the caretakers would beat me down while I yelled and cursed at them, trying to hit them back. If I got ahold of their hair, I would get hit exceptionally hard, and I would take delight making them madder. These scenes were absurd, but it showed how little I cared to get beaten-how used I was to getting beaten- and how much I despised and hated everyone around me. That cruel caretaker would get ahold of my ear and twist it until my whole head hurt, and slam my face onto the hard floor, putting a foot on my head, and whipping my bottom until I would be filled with rage and manage to get out from under her foot, bite her leg, and she would scream.

Off the caretaker would go, and the others too, and the whole fight would end and ensue the next day, after the bite was patched up and a million curses were said. I would to bed, knowing that I had "lost" my privilege to eat that night, probably the third or fourth time that week, my body boiling with anger.

It soon became time for us to move to another orphanage, having been at the current one for over a year. Lots of orphans had left. The older ones had now been dumped on the streets, and sometimes I met them while we were out walking. They tried to talk to us, but they were shooed away by the caretakers. They seemed to me to have become more mature. They didn't seem as sad as we all imagined them to be now having aged out of the system. They seemed calmer and not so violent. However, they all smelled of alcohol and several tried to introduce me to crack. Several showed me how to sniff glue. They were nice enough to have given us some stolen candy, because, I suppose, they felt sorry for us and knew how terrible it was being in the orphanage. On the streets, they weren't getting beat up. Some of them gave us some tips about street life: stay away from the police, steal as much food as you can because it would be a long time before you could find it again, sell everything and keep very little, try to dress like everyone else so that fewer people noticed you, and have a group of friends that would be with you everywhere. That way, when police caught you, the others could distract him and you could run away. Whatever the situation, the street urchins seemed knowledgeable about life in general, and that made them better people to me. They didn't seem so cruel.

Helga finally left. Her adopted parents had finally been able to get her. Which left me looking like a joke in front of everyone. I pretty much knew I was out of luck, and I simply came to accept the fact that I was not leaving. With the orphanage now having gotten much smaller, it became very quiet and the abuse had substantially dropped. There was an air of complacency. Less orphans meant less people to watch and worry about. I believe this is what the caretakers liked, so they did not really disturb us. In fact, they seemed to have gotten nicer. Instead of daily beatings, now it was like a beating once every three days or so. We went about our days playing outdoors in the backyard where the stone wall was. We would climb to the top and talk with the people on the other side. We also went into the old wooden house that no one lived in that was in the front of our orphanage. We played all the time, but it seemed that people didn't seem as enthusiastic as they used to be. That was when I got extremely sick. I would have a feverish illness for several weeks, and this was probably the first time in my life that I can remember not having been beaten for days on end. I lay in bed or outside on the grass while the others played. I recall going to the bathroom at one point and feeling my bottom hurting really bad. I spent a great deal of time trying to pull out something, whatever it was, because it felt like a needle was thrusted in me. I finally managed to pull it out, and it was a large piece of plastic. I had somehow swallowed it and must have gotten stuck. Indeed, I was prone to eating everything, because I was always hungry, including my own feces and whatever looked edible on the rock roads near our orphanages. This may have been the reason why I was so sick.

Within that time, charity people came in and we got Star Wars toys, which we could care less about and which we promptly lost as usual. It was also around this time when our TV was on a majority of the time and I watched endless episodes of Power Rangers and a terrible soap opera show with an old lady who looked really Italian. The news was always on. The channel for traditional Romanian music blasted throughout the day, and the radio was always on at nights, playing the current Romanian hits and classical music. Sometimes, I would go to bed early so that I could just roll my head side to side for hours in the sound of the radio, singing songs to myself while the other kids watched the Pokémon reruns in the girls' room right across the hallway. I recall once seeing a news report on the dorm TV of a young girl who had kicked a bottle down a well and she fell in it. It took forever to get her out (they had to lower someone in the well to get the person out) and I remember tossing all over my bed, scared that I would fall into a big black hole and never be found. I had so many nightmares about this that I could not sleep.

That being said, things became more peaceful, a sort of atmosphere that was really unusual. I was made by the caretakers to give them massages until two or so in the morning while they watched television, for apparently I had strong arms. In the day time, we would go in the backyard where an empty white building was and a trailer that never moved. And here we had games and raced. We would get on the trailer and pretend that we were leaving for some foreign land. All in all, though, I was usually left to myself, and here I just sat down and kicked a torn-up ball on the wall next to the white building. I would do this and sing, because I had nothing better to do. I think everyone was just kind of waiting to move again to another orphanage. After all, the inspectors had come again, shaken their heads, and left. It looked as if the inspection had failed as usual, and off we would go to another orphanage.

Then Wednesday came. I heard a lot of commotion. One of the caretakers came in very quickly in our dorm. She threw some clothes on the floor and told me to change, and to do it fast. So, I did. The clothes were much nicer. The shirt alone had a baseball logo on it, and it was yellow. Feeling that something special was going on, I put them on quickly. I was then taken to the nurse's office, where the nurse gave me a slip of paper and a piece of candy. The paper had a phone number on it. The nurse told me to call her sometime, to let her know what I was up to and how I was doing. All my toys were stuffed in my hands, and I was escorted back to my dorm, where a herd of orphans rushed at me and started yelling at the top of their lungs "Your parents are here! Your parents are here!"

I think my mind was rushing. I'm not sure what exactly I was thinking. For sure, this seemed like a miracle. I wanted to rush out and see this for myself, but the caretakers told me that I had to give everyone a hug, which I promptly did without much attachment to anyone except the old caretaker, whose hug was a second or two longer than all the others. Then, I rushed out, so overwhelmed with joy that I thought I could scream. I was going to America, like Helga. And I remember seeing two men, one in his late 30s or so, and another one, clearly much older, at the end of the hallway. And running up to them must have been the greatest moment ever. I overheard everyone begging me to come with me, quite the same way I was begging Helga to take me with her, but it was different being on the other side of things, being the one taken away versus the one watching another being taken away.

Well, there I was. There they were. I had a huge smile, it was great. They took me and we got into a taxi. We went to a McDonald's, where I got a lot of food and a toy boat. We then drove to a hotel, where my excitement was overwhelming. I felt like I was on top of the world. I had truly become a prince. I ate extremely well, and even overfilled myself with the ice-cream that was given to me; after all, I was still feeling ill from my sickness. It was all just amazing, though. We walked through the gardens in front of the hotel. Later, we left for the airport and I remember waiting for such a long time in lines. I'm sure a lot of them had to do with the visas and passports. The lines were simply huge, though, and we stayed in them for hours upon hours. The old man, I came to find out, was the younger man's father. This younger man, whose name I didn't know, was clearly my adopted father.

While these few days were amazing and confusing for me (I mean, I wasn't necessarily sure what was really going on), I was just overcome with curiosity and amazement for everything. I took both men's watches and placed them on myself. I felt like I was super rich. I even stold the taxi river's cigarette lighter, I thought it was so cool. My adopted parents had sent over some toys, most notably a Gameboy, which I found absolutely fascinating. I learned to play it and I grew bored with it. Truly, there was better things to look at and explore. In the hotel room, I was jumping with joy over everything. It was a new feeling, a sort of high uncertainty. It was this time where my mind seemed to spin rapidly, taking in everything as if it was new. Suddenly, I wasn't no one anymore. I had people who cared for me, and bought me nice things. All this was different and exciting. It is difficult to express because it's a feeling only a few people have the pleasure to experience. For me, it was life-changing, and only briefly did I think about the other kids in the orphanage. There were no more crying and screaming. No more restless nights and endless beatings. No more people to despise and hate. I was adopted. I was different now. Somehow, I had become superior, special in a way. Destined. Heroic. Full of opportunity and Great Expectations. I was no longer a boy who was no one. I was uncertain what I was, but I never gave it much thought. I remember being so excited that I was hysterically nervous.

Anyhow, we managed to finally get on a plane, and I remember sitting by a window, watching the other planes, singing a made-up song about airplanes. My adoptive father joined in, as well, as we watched the planes taking off one by one. These machines were just amazing to me. I never knew machines could fly. But then, our plane started going, and I remember looking out the window in great anticipation and awe as the land below got smaller and smaller. I was resolved to forget everything about my past life, because I was going to go somewhere different. I was so excited of the future. I recall looking back once, and seeing the tops of the mountains before I quickly turned around, happy and excited, with a huge smile on my face.

AFTERWARD

-

Whereas I Discuss my time Spent with my Adoptive Parents
§

After writing my memoir of my time spent in the Romanian orphanages, I became weirdly at odds of discussing my time spent in the institutions anymore. I became tired somehow; this was partly due to how people often reacted to my young life. Additionally, they would want a follow up. What happened afterwards? What was it like to be adopted, grow up adopted, and be where I wanted to be? Anyone who took considerable pity on me knew one or two things about orphanages, and most conceived that I was quite broken somehow. How did I live with that? They would follow up with these kinds of questions, and in all fairness, these questions deserve to be answered. It is my hope that this short essay will answer these questions. I am, however, more certain that more questions will be raised than answered after the work will be concluded.

It is true that when I was adopted, I came with many issues. Obviously growing up in an orphanage is not a preferable way of existing by any means, so it makes sense to conclude that I was affected in detrimental ways. I was, for example, a clumsy child. I stumbled in my words, having to take several years of speech therapy in school. I was often uncoordinated and had unheard of energy levels the like which is rare in a child. I was later diagnosed with a host of disorders such as ADHD, PTSD, Reactive Attachment, Personality Disorder, and a bunch more. I am not sure how many of them fared out as I got older, but there it was. As a child, I didn't really have much say in how I was being observed or analyzed. A great deal of people often made a lot of guesses about my past, my behavior, and my future success. It was often presumed that I was a doomed child: I was known to be intelligent, but my school grades didn't show for it (due to constant detentions and bad grades) and neither did my behavior (I was a horrid kid). Given my diagnoses, it was also assumed that I was socially inapt and could not function correctly due to my behavior and my inability to understand social etiquette.

My adoptive parents did not see any of my successes until many years after I left their home. That's because after they adopted me, my belligerent behavior turned their peaceful home into one of stress and hellish frustration. I was hardly obedient, always destructive and obstructive, I lied often and I stold more, I was always trying to be clever, and, worst of all (at least to my mother), I was extremely annoying. I had a way of irritating people because I was so overwhelming. I knew how to get under people's skin; it was actually my best ability- instigating others. The reason why I was so effective at this was largely because I had a really good social understanding of people: I have a psychological sense for peoples' weaknesses and intentions. This is an inherent skill learned from years of living in hostile environments.

My parents were well-to-do. In my mind, coming from absolutely nothing, my parents were wealthy and even noble. They had an established legacy and were respected members of society. Incorporating into their family should have been easy, but for someone like me it never was. A large reason for this is the fact that I was taken out of my homeland. This is a circumstance that, for a large majority of my life, I often downplayed, but it can never be dusted under the rug. Being adopted to a foreign land with no connection for the native land is hard. I lost my entire culture- how I talked, how I laughed, how I interacted, how I danced and had fun, and how I ate. Everything about me was shattered when I came to the United States. Having little to no knowledge of who I was, why I desired, where I came from, and why I ended up in orphanages made it very difficult to understand many things. On top of this, I lost within a year my entire Romanian vocabulary completely. I am not sure how this happens, but in my case, I completely forgot it. I became thus extremely alienated, a foreigner in a foreign land and a foreigner in my native country of birth. I somehow managed to carry over my way of speaking and thinking into English, but otherwise a major part of my young identity was shattered.

Being who I am, I am often a person who often doesn't worry about the present issues, trying to do my darnest to just make it through and make the best of whatever situation comes along. I was not very forgiving to myself as a child, no matter how much I complained. I disregarded my time spent in orphanages as just a state of life, not something to dwell too much upon. I often believed as a child that I was legimately a bad child. Perhaps I was just born this way or simply broken to the core. I believed very firmly that I was unable to ever achieve anything. I was constantly surrounded by people who did not blink an eye in describing to me, in vivid detail, how messed up I was as a child.

Two things stand out as a child living with my parents. The first is what I term my "emotional ignorance". As a kid, I always had uncertain and unpredictable mood swings. These different emotional outbursts were quickly followed by quick and impulsive reactions. The time it took for me to feel something to the point where I committed an action was very short. I often felt powerless in controlling my behavior at home and at school. When the teacher tried to discipline me, I had an immediate outburst. I threw my desk. Of course, I was sorry later, but no one cared about my sorry excuses. In fact, I often said sorry so many times that it didn't mean anything anymore. Contrary to what many people have said, I was often sorry as a kid. I was unable to manage my emotions and felt incapable of controlling myself in my moments of passion. For this reason, many therapists recommended that I needed to be retrained and basically had to restart my childhood.

My parents are by all means very good people, with the best intentions at heart. However, my mother specially could not handle me and would often read any book that might help her make me a better child. It is the unfortunate case that at these difficult moments, especially in such a delicate position that I was in, the recommended literature often states that kids like me need hard discipline. My mother was adamant in going about these recommendations with severity. Some of the things which I was accustomed to later doing: being watched while going to the bathroom, having an alarm clock upon my door, having to do morning exercises accompanied by therapeutic yoga-like movements, being rocked every morning on the rocking chair, being talked to like I was a five-year-old, placing me in my room for days and hours at a time in isolation, not having anything to do but color children's books or write in my journal. As my mother progressed in enacting these policies, my behavior became more difficult, and this meant that I was treated more severely. The days in my room in utter isolation lasted weeks and months on end. Instead of eating at the kitchen table with everyone, I was often placed in the kitchen corner and had to eat by myself. Sometimes, I would only eat bread, cheese, and water until I could "earn" better food with better behavior. I could not really exercise or stand up unless I was told to do so. I had to hold my mother's hand everywhere when she went shopping or outside. As the years rolled on and my mother's patience got thinner, my behavior became worse and the punishments became stricter. My bedroom was stripped of furniture, the window was walled up with black cardboard so that I couldn't look out, my bed was taken out and only a mattress remained. A fan was placed near my door so no one could hear me because I was so annoying. The severity of these punishments, due in large part to my rebellious nature, had a psychological traumatic toll on my brain.

Don't get me wrong, my parents never wanted to hurt me. I don't even think they knew they were causing me so much personal pain. Even if I told them how frustrated I was, they never took me seriously. They were only listening to therapists who had recommended that I be treated this way. I am unsure of whether my mother even approved some of the measures she was doing, but she rarely questioned the expertise of therapists and counselors, many of whom believed that I was severely traumatized and had no ability to be human because the orphanage had made me incapable of feeling or reasoning like a good social person. This is the popular theory of adopted kids from Eastern European orphanages, and so the idea goes that kids from these places need to be retrained and treated with as much severity and discipline as is meaningfully possible so that they can at least learn to behave correctly. As there is no "cure" for Reactive Attachment Disorder, the best that can be done to a kid, so the theory goes, is for parents to basically make these kids learn to be socially acceptable. Again and again, I was constantly reminded that I was not "fixable". I was only being trained to act properly. I wasn't human and could not understand human connection.

It is important, of course, not diminish the severity of my behavior. I did many awful things as a child, depending on whom you asked. I often lashed out at my parents, I sexually abused my sister by fondling her when she was nine and I was twelve, I would do disgusting things like pee out of my window or steal my grandmother's golden watch as she lay bedridden after surgery, and so on. The list goes on and on, and probably the best person to ask about these various and insidious behaviors is my adoptive mother, for she seemingly had a perfect memory of all these incidents as verification for the punishments that she would lay out. It goes to show how difficult my situation was for both my parents and I.

Notably, I phased into a second period in my life I call "emotional sensitivity" after the age of twelve or so. In this period, as I was going through puberty, I became extremely sensitive to everything. I felt a great deal of shame and guilt about everything. I was constantly embarrassed and reserved.

My shoulders would hunch, I avoided eye contact from everyone, every sarcastic comment towards me I took personally, and I felt incredibly paranoid about how I was being perceived. My behaviors, which were often daily matters of life, took more monthly concessions. I would be obedient for a month or so and would do something drastic that would land me in a moment of madness and, later, further punishments. My patience for my parents' punishments wore very thin. I began to have physical outbursts and would become violent. I was no longer caring about my physical wellbeing; I would react with great anger. I came to hate my parents and saw them as legimately evil people who were bent on pursuing my misery. As I lashed out more, the punishments became increasingly more severe, and it is within this time that some of their tactics became questionable and even inhumane. I was going through self-discovery and was coming to think more of my independence and personal desires, and my parents hindered every imaginable process. My attraction to girls and socializing with them was immediately prevented; my mother told all the teachers at the schools I went to that I was not allowed to speak with any girl unless for school purposes. I was prevented from joining any clubs or participating in any type of extracurricular activity. Every now and then, I would participate in something exciting, like taking piano lessons, but whenever I committed a terrible act, it was immediately withdrawn. As a result, I was often at loss what to do with myself. I was always alone and miserable, and felt these things very intimately.

To make matters worse for me, I had three older brothers and one sister who were a constant reminder of my inaptitude. My brothers had access to wonderful things-literally whatever they wanted. They went to elite Jesuit or private high schools. They had computers and wonderful digital gadgets I only dreamed of getting. One of my brothers had a beautiful girlfriend, and this often brought me great personal dismay, as I was madly infatuated with a girl at school whom I could not even talk to because I simply wasn't allowed to talk to any girls. My younger sister was the adoring child in the family, and I often despised her for receiving better treatment than I. In fact, after I had sexually abused her when I was 12, and was later told upon to my mother, I lashed out and said, quite convincingly (and I meant it) that it was a shame that I only fondled her. What I ought to have done, looking at my mother directly in the eye, was to rape her. That way, I deserved their full-blown wrath. I was demonically pleased with her horrified expression, and it only instilled in her the belief that I was incredibly inhuman somehow.

In this second period, I really did become demented and perverted. My internalization of my pain and frustration, coupled with incredibly low self-esteem and emotional sensitivity, proved to be perfect material for someone who could grow up to be insane and a horrible human being. Except that, mainly through accident, this did not truly come to be. Desiring not to have anything to do with me, my mother allowed me the ability to read books. I therefore devoured books as a child, and it pleasantly worked out for both of us. I kept quiet while she was at peace. Since books contained knowledge, my mother could see the benefit of me reading without her having to teach me anything (as I was often homeschooled given my erratic behavior) and so therefore I read hundreds of books and was not often limited from doing so. Books did not necessarily prevent me from continuing to have issues, but they did assist me in correcting a great deal of my behavior.

Books were my salvation in large part because they did something no one else could; they helped me realize what I was going through. Most of the books I read as a child were children's works, and so not very noteworthy. But sometimes, I would stumble on great classical literature and I would enter a world of incredible introspection. The first book that did it for me was Charles Dicken's *Great Expectations*. This book changed my life. It was found purely by accident at a massive open air garage sale (which my mother and I often attended in the summers- some of the happiest moments of my life). I finished the book in two days and came head-to-head with its protagonist, Pip, in ways I never conceived anywhere in my whole life. Pip had a similar life, and more importantly, Pip described in *minute* detail the very things I felt about myself and the world. I could not believe that a person 200 years earlier felt the same way, and could relate it so perfectly. And it made me feel better. I had some vocabulary to what I was feeling. The feeling that Gregor Samsa had when his mother came into the room after he turned into an insect, the fear he had of being seen and of being an inconvenience, this was called *shame*. And I felt the same exact way. The way Pip felt so deluded by Estella, no matter his infatuation, was called *dejection*. And I felt the same exact way. It was around this time when I realized that classical literature was actually the kind of books I came to understand more deeply, having considerably more depth, introspection, and emotional sensitivity. I devoured any and all I could get my hands upon, and given their length and size, my mother would only assume that this meant me being quiet only a day or two longer, as I was a fast and veracious reader.

As much as books came to help me, however, it was not the cure to my problems and my behaviors. Eventually, as I became more personally independent, and (through books) became to question the motives and behavior of my parents, I became more violent. And so, as all things come to be, in August of 2010, at the age of 16, I had a confrontation with my mother that led to a fight with my dad, the result being that I broke my father's rib, was arrested and taken to a psyche ward, and later dropped off at a children's institution many hours away from my home. In a matter of a few months, my father and mother went to court and released parental custody over to the State of Missouri. I therefore became a Ward of the State, akin to an orphan, again.

The situation I had with my adoptive parents is the unfortunate, and often the dark side, of adoptions that people often don't consider. It happens a great deal more than people know, and it is terrible for both parties. For parents who adopt, the uncertainty, frustration, and over-exhaustion of dealing with a child with myriad issues spanning both physical, mental, and linguistic, is unbearable. Therapy is costly and there is no real support for people who adopt. Many parents were not aware of all that adoption would entail. It was a life decision that ended up going array. The intention was almost always good: provide the necessities and love that a child requires, be a parent to an unwanted child, and give opportunities not afforded back in the native country to a kid who had little chance to make it in life. The problem, however, is much deeper and more complex. Some kids truly are deprived, but the unfortunate truth is that those kids are not being adopted. Kids like me were the best of the lot in a way. We were energetic, could speak well, and be as physically capable as meaningfully possible. We may have had physical and mental issues, but many parents bypassed those because we met many other requirements, such as being healthy and being classified as intelligent. No one adopts broken children; when filing papers, parents get to choose the best available child on hand. For this reason, most kids in need are really left behind. The ones that are adopted are the best available or the easiest to obtain. This often comes with a higher price tag. My younger sister (not related to me by blood), who was adopted from Bucovina, was quicker to adopt and considerably cheaper (by far). However, she was younger and considered mentally disabled. She was technically speaking a very unwanted child, and no effort was truly made to prevent her adoption. However, I was always signaled out for adoption because I was always considered extremely healthy and very smart. My energy, my "leader of the group" appearance made me a very likely candidate for adoption, and when my parents saw me, all they wanted to do was adopt me as soon as possible. Little did they know that many other families were equally just as adamant to adopt me, families from all over the world numbering into the dozens.

But when my American family did adopt me, as does happen with other kids, the situation became sour really quick. Given my age, I came with a host of problems, many deeply ingrained within me. Whereas my sister came when she was young, I came twice as old and considerably more experienced. While she was deprived from attention and clamped onto anyone who gave it to her, I was repulsed by people that wanted to get close to me. Whereas she could hardly speak or make much movement when first adopted, I came fully equipped with excellent verbal skills and vocabulary, an incredible amount of energy and movement and love for doing anything and everything, being so overwhelming to people that they became almost frighten to be around me. I could not sit still, be still, act still, or even think calmly about anything. Like many adoptive children from abroad, I was explosive and destructive. Moving into a family that was settled, calm, and reasonably happy, I turned their household upside down and made them go through mental *hell*. This is the reality. It's unfortunate, but this is what happened. When going to court to release parental custody, my parents specifically mentioned the fact that I had psychologically traumatized them. As weird as that sounds, this is truly the effect I had on them.

When placing blame, which is something that most people desire to do when in the face of injustice, outrage is usually directed towards the adults. In this case, my parents left the situation many tens of thousands of dollars less, shamed, and criticized. I can't ever dictate my story living with them without people making them out to be somehow inhumane for what they did. The idea is that, as parents, they should know better because they were adults. But the reality is that they tried everything: therapy, homeschooling, recommended polices by therapists and experts, change of lifestyle...and still, I did not improve. In the end, having exhausted all their efforts, they had to come to a very dire circumstance: does Nicolae stay or does Nicolae go? As is reasonable to do in any circumstance, given that I was the problem, I was given away. The facts could not deny that it was I who caused the issues at home, the one who made my family suffer considerably, and the one who chose, time and time again, to refuse any type of assistance.

There comes a time when the victim can no longer remain the victim anymore. I cannot cry about the fact that I was an orphan, I had been traumatized, I had problems because so and so reason. At the age of 16, I was way beyond this. No longer was I hungry, no longer was I being abused. I was now the perpetrator, the one who caused abuse, and I had completed a circle that had begun since I was a child. At the age of 16, I came to realize that I had become the very thing I had hoped I wouldn't become. But because I was always angry and vicious, incapable of expressing myself and being understood, I dug down and became demented and more disillusioned. When I was summoned to the Clinical Director's office and told my parents gave up parental custody of me, I was horrified. When I read the paper detailing why, I could only stare at it with bewilderment. The word "traumatized" had an almost damning utterance to my mind. I was no longer the child that needed help anymore. I was now a criminal. I had committed harm. This sudden realization changed me, and all the anger I ever had as a young teen swelled and disappeared within seconds.

Whereas I Discuss my Time in State Care
§

We have now come to one of the most unpleasant parts of my life. I was initially very surprised by my transition from my family home into an all-boys cottage in an institution. I found the environment similar to what I had known in Romania, and I understood now that things were probably going to revert back to that kind of world. And, unsurprisingly, it did. In a way, it was like a second chance in the orphanage system, and this time, I was a great deal more mature and better suited to the lifestyle. Being away from home was very beneficial to me in many ways because I was left alone and could dictate how much I could do within reason. I was able to learn how to play sports and could entertain myself by talking to kids who had similar problems as I had. On top of this, I realized that I could pick up new hobbies since I had a lot of time on my own. I therefore doubled my effort in reading and asking questions.

Living in an institution, however, did not solve any of my problems. The novelty of the new environment wore off and I was left in a place which provided me with a grim view of myself and the world I lived in. The fact of the matter was that, having now been a Ward of the State, I became irrelevant to everyone again. My concerns were in competition to hundreds of others. My therapy sessions were brief and not very meaningful. My medical number- No. 2467- was my ID for everything, and I was called by this number everywhere I went. When I was stressed or upset for any reason, I was never listened to and my mental and physical condition were often ignored. Many of the caretakers who took care of us worked part-time and were either psychology students or (often) military members. For this reason, we either got caretakers who cared too much or who cared too little. Based on whomever we had every day, it was either tons of push-ups, hikes, being screamed at, or days where we sat around, played sports, and fooled about. Being in these institutions is a book in itself because a great deal of things occurred and very little stayed the same for any considerable time. Stability was the desired outcome, not the reality. Kids came and went, and staff would be so overwhelmed by the job that they would stay a few weeks and disappear the following months.

The irony of the US foster care system is that there are loads of money poured into it, and yet there is so much inefficiency. I had a personal case worker (CW) who took care of my basic needs, a juvenile detention officer (DJO) who ensured I didn't go to jail and stayed within proper behavior, a guardian ad litem (GAL) who was my legal parent by law and who represented me in court, and a personal therapist (PT) in whatever institution I went. On some occasions, several other people were added, including a family therapist, a psychiatrist, an educational advisor, and various other people. Every year, I was given sexual, physical, and psychological evaluations to determine my current state of being. It was at this time where I was diagnosed with various disorders. Right and left, so many things were being done to me, per the court's order, to ensure the "best interests of the child" was being met. I was being fed double servings because I was not within my heathy weight, I had to go to therapy sessions to work on my "intimacy" since I struggled getting physically close to people, I was constantly evaluated for my mental condition and was given many different types of medication. The care was laughable; everything was a write off and could be easily manipulated. Once I told my psychiatrist that I struggled getting along with people and found everyone "stupid", hence the reason for my belligerent behavior. That person, having seen me for scarcely 10 minutes before calling the next medical number, diagnosed me with Asperger's. In another meeting, a new psychiatrist diagnosed me with insomnia because I struggled sleeping due in part to the number of medications I was receiving. This was always the answer in State Care; if a child struggles, medicate the kid until he or she is incapable of doing much of anything.

My life centered on getting used to adjusting to an everchanging environment of feelings, people, and locations. It's not an ideal world for any kid to live and grow in, but this was the reality I had to come to terms with. I was often mentally lost at this moment of my life, trying to control whatever I could but finding that I actually had little control over anything. Depression was a big part of my life at this stage; I often felt lonely and unwanted. This was exacerbated by the fact that often, kids would come to the cottage and leave within a month or two. Most of these kids were not permanent State kids in the true sense of the word. Almost all courts aim for reunification with family, and so therefore kids are highly encouraged to behave better and, in family therapy, resolve any issues they had at home before returning back.

Although reunification was also stated in my court documents as the ultimate end to my time in State Care, my mother and father had no intention of taking me back. They were going to ride the system out, hoping that I would receive the best therapy meaningfully possible.

The unfortunate truth was a lot darker behind the Ward of the State veil. The reality was that most of my personal team had no idea what to do with me. My behavior improved significantly when in institutions, and I often progressed with superior results. I proved the smartest kid in school, the best-behaved in my cottage, and the most ambitious child in probably the whole State of Missouri. There was little my team really had to say against me. But as I was "living" in State Care, another problem began to brew in the court: my parents and my grandparents. Since coming to the US, I had managed, through my behavior, to alienate and pull apart many of my mother's and father's friends and family members who disagree over how my parents tried to discipline me. They found my mother's reaction overreaching and even inhumane. They belittled my father, whom they called weak and passive. My mother was considered cruel and overbearing, a "helicopter" parent. My mother's parents were especially critical of my mother, and so since I was a young child, their relationship had soured considerably. She would refuse to talk to them, refused to come to their house or take us there, or even to meet for special occasions like Thanksgiving and Christmas. My grandparents, realizing that they may have erred, tried to take family therapy, but nothing worked. My grandparents continued to question my mother's tactics and behavior, and eventually, in time, my mother-feeling greatly unsupported and hurt by their suspicions-refused to cooperate with them unless in certain situations. The irony with this situation was that the same way she felt about her parents is exactly the same way I felt towards my mother.

After being placed in State Care, my grandparents stepped into my life and became, legimately, what I would term my "true" parents. I became especially close to my grandfather, who was understanding and who actually saw my rebellious behavior as a normal way of growing up, since he had done many similar things as I. He understood my ambition, my distasteful behavior, and my incredible frustration and anger at the world. My grandmother, being something of my mother but a great deal wiser and more nurturing than my mother ever was, was adamant that I succeed no matter the cost. Without question, she would happily buy me any book I desired. I had a collection of hundreds of books and she tried to salvage my childhood by taking me to movies and nice dinners. Their commitment was unreal: every week, they'd drive two hours to my institution down south to see me for half a day before driving back two hours. They'd spend thousands of dollars on me through entertainment, books, and new experiences. My grandma ensured that I always had my haircut, got new clothes, and that I was well fed. And they did it in such a way as if to say, "don't worry about it, we want to do this for you". My grandparents became such an important part of my life that I actually came to believe they were my true team, the only people who really cared for me. And legally, they were technically not even my grandparents. In this sense, then, they became benefactors for me. Their support was so strong that many of the kids who often met them would remark how amazing they were and how jealous they were to not have people like them in their lives. However, my situation was actually not very new. Many State kids had grandparents who obtained a whole new meaning in life by coming weekly to see their grandchildren, and, like my grandparents, take the kids out to do entertaining things. I would often come back from my visits incredibly discouraged by their absence and couldn't wait to see them again. I would literally stare out the cottage windows in anticipation of their arrival- like a kid.

After being placed in State Care, my parents initially did not really care to see me or have anything to do with me. Things moved pretty fast and the court tried to determine a quick route for me to become socially independent and transition into society as efficiently as possible. They saw my grandparents as the means to do this, as they offered to take me in and raise me as one of their own kids. With my grandparents' backing, I could actually go to high school and later college. However, for an uncertain reason I am unsure of, my parents stepped into the picture again and were against any such move. My mother stated she was worried about my grandparents' health and safety, prompting inspections of their background and their home. Given the fact that, although not legally my parents anymore, my parents had the "right" to sit in court and state their opinions given their status as my parents, they resumed a place in my life that would hinder much of my progression in State Care. On top of this, the judge assigned to me was a good friend of my mother and father and I could not help but think that this aspect only played to their favor. I had a whole team and not one of them took me seriously. However, when my parents spoke, their word was taken seriously because my mother "knew" me the best. As such, I was often put in the back seat and watched as things swirled around me with little control over my destiny. Incredibly, even though they gave up their custody over me, my parents held a lot of control over my life, questioning everything and being flustered that I wasn't getting what I needed in terms of therapy or discipline. My team listened to them and would often enact their wishes without my consent on anything. My relationship with my parents got to the lowest point when they championed my move from a level 2 facility to a level 4+ institution (effectively juvenile detention).

The stalemate in court, as my parents and grandparents fought for what they thought was a better way to take care of me, led me to become very frustrated. My caseworker was also coming down with some serious health issues and was often incapable of taking care of me, which left me extremely alone and incapable of being heard. My team was an utter failure in many regards, and I wasn't really alone in this. Many kids experienced the same issue. Their teams lacked cohesion, a solid plan, and much motivation to stir the pot and get things going. I would sit in my cottage, having achieved all the criteria I needed to achieve to get out of the institution only to be told to be patient for months and years on end as someone figured out what to do with me. I would see kids finish their assigned court programs only for me to look at myself and be incapable of escaping this prison-like environment. I quickly found out that the only way my team would ever truly respond to me was by commiting a serious crime or outburst, a tactic I used sporadically to my advantage.

In State Care, I only committed two serious crimes worthy of prison; both of them took place on a computer, in a school setting, and both resulted in expulsion from school. Both relate to porn and accessing websites that were highly illegal (or would be if the law knew they existed). There was suspicion that I had hacked computers and school systems, and therefore proved dangerous. Because both instances were sexual in nature, a constant fear swirled amongst my team that I was sexually deviant and possibly a predator in the making. The first crime led me to be removed from my first institution and sent packing to a place far in the countryside where rules were more lenient and we kids were treated like kids. I was able to interact and have fun with others my age, and even able to mingle with girls. My happiest teen years was spent there, in that cottage, in the middle of the forest. We were often told to act like family members and be supportive of one another, to the point where we had to eat together for meals. Given that we were often left alone, we had to devise our own things to entertain ourselves. For this reason, I picked up roller skating, riding bicycles, and playing sports like pool, football, and basketball. We went to summer camps in ranches and took excursions out to places all over the state. Best of all, I was able to obtain an mp3 player and be able to indulge in classical music and playing video games on the PlayStation in the basement. Every Friday, us boys would go down and watch a movie.

This situation went pretty well for me for about half a year and a little more. However, it was short-lived. Most of the great cottage staff left (as they were often students at the nearby S&T University), many of the kids I had bonded with went back home to their families, and suddenly younger and younger boys came in our cottage. Down at the local school for us State Kids, things became insane. Teachers couldn't teach as fights would break out every day. I recall our teacher having to have a security guard in order for him not to get beat up, and me reading The Princess of Mars while a whole squad of black kids were beating up a gay black kid for exposing the fact that he was gay and was sexually attracted to one of the boys in the class. It only took one person getting into a fight before everyone would rush out of their seats and try to get involved. Everyone was on edge, always desperate to join a brawl and always excited to beat up anyone else they hated or had any type of beef with. The chaos that ensues in the school was legendary; some of the things I encountered were unbelievable even for me, and I had seen a lot of things the year before in Columbia's facility.

My understanding of State Care was greatly increased in St. James (the city of my second institution). Boredom, chaos, and emotional overreaction was the norm wherever I went. It fed the institutions like wood to a fire. Kids never improved. I rarely saw any kid truly become better in these homes. If anything, they enforced high levels of aggression and the ever-arching philosophy that people don't care about you. Nothing was ever resolved in State Care, and the rule was everything just needed to be put aside in hope that the problem would go away. Only when the issues escalated to severe violence was anything done; here, I was met with a raw and ugly reality. Given that us kids were older, much of our violent behavior was rarely acceptable without severe consequences. In times like these, the institution would call the police and the person would be arrested. Tons of kids would therefore be arrested and be sent to jail for being violent. It was around this time where the ¾ concept was readily being stated, almost amusingly, at every therapy event. The ¾ idea was that 3 out of 4 State or Foster kids would end up in jail after leaving institutions- this was based on some kind of statistic. I'm unsure of its accuracy, but I believe it since every kid in State Care knows many others who went to prison. In fact, the success rate for most kids is so abysmally low that it was often a shock if a kid ever left the system and went to community or technical college.

With this in mind, I felt like my future was somehow in jeopardy. All around me was chaos and uncertainty, and my team hardly considered anything meaningful for me. I kept trying to think how to secure my future, whether this was Transitional Living or the military. I never considered college because I knew I didn't have enough money (in fact, I had none at all). I also didn't believe I was smart enough to go to college, no matter how arrogant I was. It was true that school was easy. Teachers often left me alone to read books while they continued teaching multiplication to 16- or 17-year-old kids. State kids were so uneducated that many teachers had a hard time helping those who were more intelligent or better educated. For this reason, some would bring in books for me to read. Luckily for me, I had cracked open in the basement of our cottage a forgotten room which proved to be a library of thousands of untouched and unread books- many of whom were classical literature. In the span of a year, I was immersed to Greek, Roman, Victorian, and French literature. My knowledge improved vastly, able to now comprehend historical and social events with a vivid mind. I overtook my teachers and could speak on difficult topics such as philosophy, art history, and psychology. On top of this, being immersed in black and latino culture helped me stay out of my intellectual bubble; after reading Suetonius, for example, I would go and do freestyle raps with the others "on the Hill" (a term we used to refer to those on the other side of the forest), and afterwards meet the hipster kids and work on fixing bikes.

My true personality was somewhat formatted at this young age. Before, I was quite timid and bewildered about everything. But when I came to my second institution, I began to think considerably more and became more calculating. I thought through my actions, wondering how I could avoid situations and how to get people to either leave me alone or get me things I wanted. I wasn't manipulative in the sense that I wished to do wrong, I was manipulative in the sense that I had a strong ego and belief in my superiority over others and wanted to prove it no matter what. I was rather combative in my approach, and this was seen as somewhat respectable since I followed a more chivalrous approach in having arguments or being aggressive. I knew I was smarter than everyone, and I also knew that I was a great deal more ambitious and motivated than others. Once I was recognized as brilliant, I assumed a leadership role wherever I went and became the dominant figure amongst my peer group.

However, when people questioned me or tried to fight me, I used my sarcasm and instigative nature to undermine them and I proved very successful at this. Given my stature (after all, I was 5'6 and weighed scarcely 125 pounds), I couldn't beat up anyone, and I know, having been beaten up a few times in my time in State Care. Therefore, to adapt, I developed a very spiteful and demeaning tone and became an excellent "mind-shifter", as they said. Basically, if I didn't like anyone for whatever reason, I would tell someone what I thought of them and back it up with a hundred different examples, flooding them with a bad perception of them. In the end, I would tell the person that it was just my opinion in order for them to perceive that I wasn't trying to sway their opinion when in reality I very much was. Given my reputation as a diplomatic and intelligent fellow, people would assume that I couldn't be wrong about my analysis and almost always sided with me. In the end, then, I would win the person over and the person I didn't like would be in the inconvenient position of being disliked and distrusted by everyone. Almost certainly I overplayed my description of the person I didn't like, but it didn't matter to me at the time as I perceived that by having allies, I was safe and should I ever be attacked, tons of kids would come to my aid. This tactic was very effective for me, and saved me many times. For this reason, I was known as a troublemaker and an instigator, but with little regard to it, as I was also seen as a person with high potential and a good heart. Whenever people did want to fight me or get me in trouble, I had the support of the staff and my peers throughout. Very few people ever questioned me or my intentions, and so therefore I continued to learn and become more adaptive. Nevertheless, I loved to help people, and I was keen in assisting others when they needed help with anything.

This experience made me believe that I was suited best to become a politician, and so it became the running joke that one day I'd become a senator or a president (of Romania). I was seen as highly ambitious, a good socializer, and an excellent bullshitter. On top of this, I was deemed the smartest kid around and incredibly adaptable. This was so even when my school grades were handed out. As usual, I never did well in school (though better than most), but I never cared for school. I always thought school was boring, tedious, and very simple. My arrogance increased as I read more and found everyone around me to be even dumber than I had realized. It turned up one or two notches when I began to be awarded things: I was awarded twice the Good Samaritan medal at the Meramec Adventure Camp (meant like a summer therapy camp for State Kids) for always assisting people completing tasks and Person Most Likely to Succeed in school. My leadership was unquestioned, and my eccentric behaviors were passed over with a degree of indifference. I never gave anyone problems and I was given as much liberty as feasibly possible. In this way, I actually started to have fun.

However, all things that begin end soon enough. Many of the kids left, I went back to feeling like nothing was happening, and I became miserable again. The cottage I was in began relocating State Kids and taking in "insurance kids", which are kids that come in for a small time to shape up and have better behavior, sort of like the idea of Scared Straight where kids go see what prison looks like for a day. These kids would only last a week or two before leaving and loving the fact that they had parents, promising to be better. I would see parents literally in tears as they would drop their kids off, unable to bear "giving them away" for one or two weeks, which wouldn't take much of an imagination to know how I perceived that. My parents, to sweeten the deal, came to visit me and were flabbergasted by my easy and casual lifestyle, where I could stroll anywhere, play videogames, and do what I pleased. They complained to my Case Worker that I was "goofing around" like I was on vacation, and this began a movement in my team to reconsider if I was really being treated for my issues, which was a whole list down, according to my medical papers.

In court, an assessment was made about me; I needed to work on my sexual deviancy and therefore needed to relocate to a place that dealt with these issues. Having found no place available, it was determined that I would need to go to the only place that would accept me given my age. That place happened to be on a military base in the middle of Missouri, and it happened to also be a lockdown facility, level 4+, equivalent to juvenile detention. I had heard of this place as the hell hole for the worst kids and I tried to argue my way out of going there, but my abrupt behavior in court was considered suspicious. My parents argued that I had to go because my sexual deviancy was a real issue and didn't care whether I didn't want to go there or not. My case worker couldn't locate another place for me, so this one she deemed as the only available place for me to go. My lawyer was absent and a fill-in was offered who made no real effort to support me. My grandparents, having gone there days before, noted that the place was truly bad, but their assessment was derailed because my medical papers were reevaluated and the incident with my sister from age 12 was recounted, as well as the incident I had at my previous institution where I was expelled, and so thus...my DJO got involved and was all for me relocating as soon as meaningfully possible. This swayed the judge considerably (since my DJO never said anything, given my good behavior), and so I was immediately sent to a place called Piney Ridge Center. They referred to it as a residential treatment center; it was legimately a prison.

My cynicism in life took for the worst in Piney. I was immediately stripped and given green scrubs to wear (green was for Sexually Abusive Youth, or SAY). All my belongings were taken away and was constantly confined in small spaces in a room of 20 to 30 boys. My mental health went down as I was constantly reminded, and branded, as a sexual predator. My therapists rehashed the incident with my sister, and this became my occupation for the rest of my two years in this hell hole. My parents seemingly felt better about my situation, feeling that I was now getting "real treatment". What they didn't know was how badly I wanted to commit suicide and escape. If I had thought I had been manipulative before, I became ten times more manipulative in Piney Ridge, and for the worst, too. I became mentally and emotionally harden, coming to hate my team and my parents dearly. Being locked and supervised so meticulously made me rather insane, forcing me to have to learn how to adapt in such an extreme environment. I felt wronged and silenced and brainwashed. Everyone was keen on a set of rules: I had to admit that I was a sexual predator, I had to accept it and realize that I would always be one and that there was no cure, I had to do intense therapy and self-reflection on how bad I was as a person, and then I had to develop a relapse plan to ensure I never looked at a child or adult in a sexual way again. When I refused or showed any type of disagreement, I was immediately searched and thrown in solitary confinement, a cold white room, for days and hours on end. I would lose all privileges and have to restart treatment all over again. Given such minute control over my life, my therapist had ultimate power over where I stayed, what I did, and what my future plan looked like. No one in my team cared or knew what I was going through, and the communication between Piney and my team was minimal at best. My team only visited me once and stayed scarcely 30 minutes, never bothering to ask or cared how I was doing. Most were only concerned with ensuring that I had my clothing voucher for the year, I got my evaluations done, and that I received my medical care. Checking boxes, not how the kid is doing.

There was a moment in Piney when I felt like everyone was aiming to ruin me and ensure that I sit in some asylum room for the rest of my life. After ruminating for a long time, I came to the conclusion that, as a person, I needed to change. I needed to become a better liar, a better manipulator, a better playmaker. Having seen no one except my grandparents who cared about me, I felt that I needed to really think only of myself and my survival. I was considerably late in this game, and I realized that many of my peers had already discovered this realization. I therefore became more open to their suggestions and worked feverishly together to assume as much leadership in the place I could get and manipulate everyone accordingly. After one year of working my way to the top, committing to a relapse program, and admitting everything they wanted me to say, I managed to be relocated scarcely 10 yards away to a trailer called "The Bridge", which was a smaller place which offered a little more freedom. When I left Piney, my relief was immense. If I could have burned down the place, I most definitely would have. Piney taught me, above all, that bad things happen regardless of what you desire or want to happen. It taught me that people are always being dealt unfortunate hands, and often wrongly. It taught me to stop feeling sorry for me, that I needed to become personally tougher, and that people play power games and let their egos go to their heads in their pursuits to be right all the time and in control of everything- at the expense of anyone in their way. Piney made me realize that what I did to my sister 6 years before, I was paying for now in a prison-like environment. I have never spoken to my sister since that day when I was 12, so I have no idea if she continues to hate me or wonder if I am doing well. Whatever the case, if she forgot that incident, I most certainly have not. It has stayed with me and ensured that wherever I went in State Care, I was branded as a pedophile and a sexual predator.

At the Bridge, I continued much of my cynicism and went back to my hobbies, playing sports and reading books. I did so a changed person, very much harden and skeptical. My parents became meaningless to me, I came to have a stronger relationship with my grandparents, and I began to focus on how to get out of Piney (since the "Bridge" was also part of Piney). In the meantime, I plotted an escape for one of the kids inside the facility who knew he was going to be stuck there for years on end if he failed his sexual evaluation. I began to manipulate people into doing my "dirty work" in instigating others or doing petty things like stealing from the kitchen or other people's rooms. Although most of the staff was well-aware that I was always thinking up ways to do things and masterminded these stupid acts, they couldn't prove it was me directly, so I was always watched with a great deal of suspicion. It took the supervisor of the "Bridge" to sit me down and directly tell me that I was developing a mobster-like mentality; I needed to focus on doing what I needed to do to get out of the place. However, I knew better. If I ever acted correctly, people would just ignore me and continue to assume I had the patience to wait around and hold out. I was already 19 years of age, and I hadn't moved anywhere in my life. I therefore decided that I had to commit one very serious act for things to change and for me to be reevaluated.

At this point in my life, school was the issue at hand. At 19 years of age, I was in my second year of high school when I should have been graduated. That was thanks to my mother, who had kept me back a grade when I was first adopted, and again when I was in fifth grade (perhaps as an insult, or perhaps because I never learned anything that year). The problem was that I was already educationally superior to everyone by that age- so much so, I said, that I could go directly to college. No one believed me when I mentioned this, largely due to my average grades which were in line to everyone else's. This was especially true because in school, I often disregarded schoolwork and just went directly to the tests. In practice, it looked like I couldn't muster sitting in class for long hours and doing homework, let alone take hours long tests to pass high school and an entrance exam for college. My status in school was the only thing that my team would refer to when dictating what my next move should be. I couldn't go to Transitional Living until I was graduated, and I couldn't leave State Care until I graduated. Therefore, school was the thing that prevented my advancement. It occurred to me that I needed to get expelled again from the school system. But it had to be something so incredibly heinous that there would be no exceptions; after all, it was a one-time action that needed quick punishment and expulsion.

It did not take me too long for me to figure out what I needed to do. I simply repeated my behavior from the high school that I got previously expelled from- I again went back on the computer, "hacked it", went on illegal websites, and accessed porn. Immediately, I was "caught". I say "caught" lightly because a massive argument began to ensue over whether I actually committed the crime. Those that knew me never could imagine I'd ever do such a thing, and those that didn't particularly like me finally found out "how much of a pervert" I was. I was immediately stripped down again, lost all my privileges, was relocated to the main facility again, sent to solitary confinement, and became suicidal again. This was short-lived, however, because I quickly found out that I was expelled from school. This became evidently clear when I was notified that the FBI was looking at my case, since I had "hacked" a school system network on military property. There was possibility of me getting arrested, charges to be filed, and for me to be thrown in prison, now that I was an adult. My team scrambled to figure out what to do. My DJO did not want me in prison and worked to get the charges dropped. My Case Worker couldn't really care less but was obligated by law to have me in school. My grandparents and parents were horrified. And my GAL, as usual, made no remark. My only new change was the fact that my judge was offered a new judicial post and I obtained a much nicer, and more empathetic, woman in his place. She was adamant that I consider a future plan for myself. She didn't care for my parents, grandparents, or Case Worker. She made me focus and evaluate what I wanted to do. When I told her that I wished to drop out of school and take the GED test to graduate out of high school early, she demanded that my Case Worker make it happen. She was adamant that I get out of the State Care system and learn to be independent as soon as possible. Her words were clear: figure it out or you're going to jail!

Having her support greatly improved my situation since I now could meet deadlines and be ready for the next step. Having gone through everything before, I simply played along and did what I was supposed to do. The new clinical director at the place decided that my therapist was incompetent in dealing with me, and decided to take me for her sessions. In the next two months, I was able to have the most meaningful discussions I ever had in my life. Her warm and affectionate demeaner caught me off guard. She exposed my closed-minded stubbornness, my reserved physical nature, and my manipulative tactics- seemingly very well aware of people like me. After enduring such a brutal attack on my character, she looked at me and told me that she knew exactly why I did these things, and began, in a very detailed manner, to tell me that I felt powerless, that people that were supposed to care for me failed in doing so, that I was often misunderstood, and that all my issues were swept under the rug since I landed in a chaotic system. I was bewildered by her assessment and honestly shocked by her thorough understanding. On top of this, she noted that I was too intelligent to "go down to these peoples' levels", that I had too much potential for me to throw away for a form of injustice I refused to let go, and that she assumed that I would become an incredible thinker one day if only I took a deep breath, looked around, became self-aware, and took control of my life. I didn't say much that day, leaving her office feeling as if she unlocked something very deep within myself. Whereas I was used to being told that I was brilliant, I had never been accessed so correctly with such acute understanding, and then told that I was meaningful to anyone. And she believed it entirely. She had said it very indifferently, as well, which means that to her, it was very obvious, and obviously true, as if she considered anyone who didn't see what she saw as too stupid not to realize it. And I felt considerably stupid, because I neither believed nor saw these things in myself. Of course, I knew I was intelligent, but I never believed it was genuine; I simply suspected that I was just an incredibly good bullshitter. It's true that I have always been a leader and often assumed such authoritive positions, but I never believed that was genuine either; I just assumed I acted this way due to my insecurity, not simply because I had those qualities. This therapist made me realize very suddenly that I was causing my own demise and that I was in complete control of myself. This is the first day in my life when I began to self-reflect genuinely. Even though she left scarcely two months later, she gave me everything I needed to move on.

   With renewed energy, I doubled in my effort and began my effort to take my GED courses. I was sent to study with a special teacher, and a few months later, I took my GED test and passed with exemplary grades. Having now completed my high school degree two years early, my judge demanded that a new plan be assessed. I did it for her; I wanted to go to college. As my Case Worker, parents, and team struggled to figure out how to make that a financial reality (since there is no help for State Kids who desire to go to college), my grandparents immediately stepped in and stated that they would pay for my education, catching everyone off guard, including myself. My grandmother saw the golden opportunity and stated that she would ensure that I stayed with her as I studied for my ACT entrance exam, and, if I got accepted, she would ensure that all my education would be paid for. My parents were against this idea, my team had no other suggestion or rebuttal, and so thus the judge ordered that I be taken out of Piney and relocated to my grandparents.

   This moment was a substantial win for me and my grandparents who fought for four years to get more control over my life and ensure that I got better education, and a massive blow to my parents, who were clearly angered and pissed beyond compare. I left Piney excited for the future and fully energized. The next few days were spent contemplating what kind of person I wished to be. I imagined how amazing college would be and what wonderful grandparents I had. Having encountered so much chaos and change in the past four years, I decided to forget all about it and refocus on a better tomorrow. I realized that my entire childhood had been ruined and miserable, but that the future looked incredibly bright and hopeful. There was a new world awaiting me; like Pip, I was bound for Great Expectations. On December 6, 2013, my grandparents came to pick me up from Piney. It was my 20th birthday.

Whereas I Discuss my Time in University
§

I took my ACT residual test at the University of Missouri-St. Louis that January of 2014 in the middle of a snow storm. I obtained entrance in the school with an overall grade of 26, which was rather mediocre and not very extraordinary. This was in large part due to my dismal grade in mathematics, which I've never been very good at. Because of this, I was immediately placed on academic probation for my first semester in college. I cared little, however, as I felt that I was now really doing something spectacular. Almost immediately, I jumped into campus activities, joining intermural soccer teams, getting initiated into a fraternity, and getting involved in student government positions. I took classes that were interesting to me, especially art history, philosophy, and political science, the degree I decided to major in. Having grandparents who took care of my finances helped me immensely; while others were taking out massive loans and complaining about paying them back, I could comfortably be assured that I did not have to worry about anything but studying.

University, however, proved to be a place of contradictions and mental frustrations. I wanted to fit into everything, so I joined every single organization I could get into. I would pour hundreds of dollars of my State Care stipend (which was around $400 some dollars) into meaningless donations and products, like a PlayStation or new laptop computers. After a year of doing these stupid things, I realized I was simply getting broke from doing this, and it wasn't helping me make better friends or better connections to anyone. In fact, my free spending made it appear that I was somewhat wealthy, and so people would randomly come up to me and ask me for money. When my fraternity had a charity event, I was the first to be called and asked to donate- for a "good" cause, of course. The reality of these initiations were far different than what I had really expected. After all, the charities were only a front for a carefully crafted image of the fraternity so it could enhance its social parties, get more members, and have more influence on campus. In student government, I realized that many of the students were only obsessed with personal ambitions and were wrapped in an ideology of social justice and being nice so as to make them appear more diverse and appealing than personally relatable. This concept was readily applicable to just about all the students on campus, and it was something that I had never encountered before. I was used to people scheming cynically in State Care, or hiding behind religious mysticism (like my parents), to advance their ambitions and personal desires. I was not used to people using public good (or in the "service of others") to ensure they could realize personal ambitions.

As a student of political science, I quickly found myself calling out people's bluff and taking particular delight in outlining, through sarcasm and witty condescending statements, how others were wrapping up their selfish positions in nice facades. I therefore quickly became unpopular in my department, being known as conservative and a staunch contrarian. I was placed in the minority camp of ideology in my department called conservatism, and was often hounded in class about my personal views in just about anything. I was always quick to note people's hypocrisy, and people were incredibly quick to note the entirety of my -isms. It was in college when I realized that I held a lot of beliefs that were against the status quo. I was racist, for example, very sexist, elitist, found democracy to be a dumb idea, and agreed on almost every hard policy imaginable on any given topic. My personal heroes were Andrew Carnegie, Napoleon Bonaparte, and Theodore Roosevelt. I was against the LGBTQ community on campus, almost always showing disapproval when funding was allocated to them in meetings, and often made fun of the African American organization. Everything anyone agreed with, I took a singular approach away from, and so therefore I became one of the most controversial figures on campus. Given that I held prominent student positions (i.e., President of the Political Science Academy, Vice-Chair of the Student Senate, Vice-President of the Associated Students of the University of Missouri System, a judge of the Student Conduct Committee, and several others), my existence proved problematic on my fronts. I realized a little time later that many of these "beliefs" and behavior were actually my way of distancing myself from superficial people; I very rarely acted according to my beliefs, and when I found myself contradicting what I would often say, much to the surprise of others, I didn't even question the reason why. I was doing what I was doing to get a rise out of people, and I was very effective at it. However, behind everyone's back, professors and students who came to know me personally found me interesting, different, and libertarian. One of my professors had mentioned that I was akin to Robespierre or General Patton, whichever was worse, knowing that I would always take the extreme side to any dilemma proposed.

The truth was that college was not at all what I thought it would be. From the books I read as a kid, I thought college was a bunch of students hanging about philosophizing on the nature of what is the proper way of living or getting to learn about the historical greats. It, in fact, was something altogether very different. It was a factory-like setting where students worked in classrooms and did just enough to pass by. The important things were tests and memorizing facts. Very rarely did anyone have an original idea or create anything amazing. I rarely met amazing people in college. Most of them were, as they term themselves, "activists" towards a "better tomorrow". This often meant hounding people that disagreed with them, actively demonizing those who held different views, and calculative measures against allowing others to freely speak their minds. In college, it was taught that students can't really share opinions on matters unless they align with very specific things. It was here when I began to consider, with minute detail, a massive work on the concept of victimization and minority, a philosophical, economic, and historical account on how people use minority status as a means of power. College did provide me with a motivation to explore many topics, however, and I was amazed at all the things I missed out on from my reading. I took every imaginable class that spiked my interest, whether that was Middle East literature, medieval architecture, Asian philosophy, Fundamentals in Acting, business ethics, anthropology and cultures, French, Philosophy of Religion, crime and genocide in history, and Inquiries into Film, besides others.

The class that had the most impact on me was a class called Existentialism, a form of philosophy that discusses, amongst other things, the purpose and meaning of life. Although I was hesitant to take this course, I was curious, and in the end, it proved to be the most influential course I ever took, changing my mind forever. After reading a work from Kierkegaard titled *Fear and Trembling*, I decided that I had to reevaluate my life and consider what exactly I was aiming to do with it. I followed up the book by reading Dostoevsky's *Underground Notes*, Heidegger's *Being and Nothingness*, and Camus's *The Stranger*, a work that seemed, line by line, to provoke the strangest, and deepest, thoughts I ever had. I looked around me and saw almost every student playing puppet roles, incapable of being truly free-thinking or even measurably intelligent, and I felt disgusted by being around such people which I began to uneasily see as idiotic, passive, and smart in knowing things but dumb in understanding things objectively. School wasn't difficult, but being around its hypocrisy proved to make me irritated and disenchanted. Having already felt this way within my first semester, I became obsessed with finishing school in two years instead of four. My grandparents found this very agreeable since it meant that they wouldn't have to spend as much money on school expenses, and I felt better because I didn't have to keep expecting, and asking them, to pay off school bills as soon as possible. In fact, in my shame due to their charity, I often refused to share with them how much money I had to pay off, and in my last semester, I took out over $10,000 in student loans instead of giving them the bill. I didn't want to be as dependent on them, especially now that I was a grown adult and over the age of 21.

The difficulty in college was also expounded by the fact that I became incredibly infatuated with a beautiful Colombian girl who shared, amongst other things, a personality of good insight and cynicism. I felt she could see things as I did and even expand on difficult topics with great subtlety. However, being so incredibly beautiful, she was occupied with numerous love affairs, deciding what to do in her future, and by the overwhelming knowledge that she was not wealthy and she was becoming older, meaning that she was becoming less beautiful and therefore not as mystical to men, whom she relied on with great understanding to further her goals. Her existence occupied a great deal of my mind, making me sluggish and miserable after being rejected when I asked to date her. Nevertheless, we remained somehow involved as friends, and this only made matters terribly worse as I was always constantly aware that she was with someone else and yet I never had the chance to be either intimate or personal with her. I tried my darnest to win her affections, even searching the whole cities of Florence, Assisi, Sorrento, and Rome to find her earrings that matched the beautiful bluish-green color of her eyes. The pain from her rejection, which, granted, was not her fault but mine entirely, made me realize how incompetent as a person I was to desire female admiration and appreciation. It only enhanced my understanding of existentialism to the point where I began to realize, ever so slowly, that living life was really a horrid and painful existence.

Having extracted all that I could from university at the age of 22, I graduated in 2016 with a BA in Political Science. I aimed, at least I thought, to become a politician in the future, perhaps relocating to Washington D.C. for my next career, perhaps as a legislative intern or even working for the office of a senator like Lindsey Graham or Roy Blunt (whom I had met a year before). However, I was quite adamant to continue with my education and at least obtain an MA degree so that I could say that I was really educated and had risen to the top of the classist society that I had always dreamed to be. In the end, I ended up getting accepted at several universities, but the one I chose was a university program done in a diplomatic academy in Berlin, Germany. I was excited to return to Europe, and I was excited to finally snap all the strings that kept me tied down from my family, courts, or my past life. I wanted to start afresh and Europe seemed like the place to do it. I went to Berlin on October of 2016. It would prove to be the next phase of my life which solidified the kind of person I ended up becoming.

Whereas I Discuss my Time Abroad
§

I came to Germany tight on money. After paying my first year of MA university early ($6,000), I came with a little less than $2,500 that was, theoretically, to last me the whole year. It would prove to be a painful and dehumanizing error. Within a few months, I was broke. In school, the education was minuscule. Everything was very different, very direct, and very unstructured. Whereas in the US, everything is catered to your educational means (large staff, massive dorms and halls, and an almost city-like infrastructure), university in Germany was far smaller, more incompetent, and less worried about your personal success. The opportunities afforded was also much less, since their departments were smaller and carried considerably less staff. Whereas my previous university held somewhere between 15 to 20,000 students (and that's considered small), my German diplomatic academy held scarcely 150 students. The place was also sketchy in the sense that infrastructure was poor, the education was not first-rate as had been proposed, and the partnerships with various universities across Europe were not upheld. I, for example, applied for a degree in Globalization in partnership with the University of Bucharest, Romania. However, I was literally the only person who applied for this program. I was technically supposed to study one year in Berlin and one year in Bucharest; in the end, being the only student in this program, I was reassigned to the University of Furtwangen and was reassigned a different degree: International Relations and Cultural Diplomacy. Although this initially pissed me off, since I felt cheated, it actually proved beneficial to my end.

My time in Berlin exposed me to an immense worldview I had never experienced before. The diversity of people, the cataclysmic clash of cultures, and the individuality of members provided me a chance to explore things one by one. Regardless of my disregard for how hard such an immersion was for me, it proved incredibly beneficial for me to encounter these things. Once again, I came with a rigid mindset full of -isms, which, to my surprise, though people hated me for them, many came to like my independent way of thinking. I therefore became, someway somehow, a personality in myself. My arrogance grew substantially, but I also came to terms with my own limitations. I was, for example, not good with money. I wasn't an eloquent speaker, and I was readily made fun of for this reason when making class presentations. My eccentric personality rubbed everyone the wrong way, and I was seen as abrasive, incredibly arrogant with nothing to prove for it, and an imposter. My ideas were easily disregarded as unacademic and my status as a student, which isn't anything in Europe, made me incapable of being noticed. Europe silenced people more than the United States, and cared little for individual uniqueness. Europeans work in systems, typically, making them more crowd-oriented than most US Americans, and for this reason, though people in Europe could think, they were highly unmotivated in life. No one aspired to greatness as in the US. They were more practical, and scornful, to ever consider themselves worthy enough to be anyone of importance. They showed enormous respect for people who were powerful, held more academic titles, and were their supervisors. In essence, Europe was very backward and pathetically outdated. What made it worse is that they recognized that they were as such, but, as they pointed out to me, European systems work, and they don't want to change that. American systems exploit, and that's the problem. The irony of this thought, though somewhat true, means that both Americans and Europeans remain victims to their fears.

I was again reminded by the fact that I was, once again, surrounded by very unmotivated and very pessimistic individuals that had little hope for the future. People who followed simplistic values and actions with little care for holistic understanding of issues. And, as for me, I was reminded constantly that I was poor and a quick spender on things that disregarded necessities, like food, for the sake of a new book. It was at this time when I seriously considered writing books, and began to first draft books on poetry and my memoir from my time in Romania. However, within a year, I became a furious writer, having a good dozen works completed before I turned 24. My interest in a variety of topics saw me contemplate works on perception of existence, the nature of German mentality, artistic decadence, several novellas, several poetic works such as plays and sonnets, and descriptive essays on philosophical ideas. I also began to travel more, using the little money I could make from the various jobs I did to see different countries and encounter different cultures. I relocated to London for a summer so that I could get a better job and make more money to pay for my second year in university. I traveled to Kurdistan so that I could be close to the Battle of Mosul while I helped a friend write a book about the Kurds. I traveled across Europe and became extremely familiar with Eastern Germany as I worked for a London-based company that updated Maps for Google.

In that meantime, I developed very strong friendships with my professor/former ambassador at school, a famous German pianist who became my tutor and mentor, and my first roommate, a German from Lower Saxony who proved the most valuable companion and friend as I endured, and explored, the world. As my life took a whirlwind of new experience into it, I became more drenched with ideas and concepts, all of which eventually ended up in the numerous piles of books I would write in a short time. My poverty became irrelevant to me, as I realized I could just travel somewhere else for work and, with my German friend, I now had someone who could manage my money in proper order. My erratic behavior, however, especially my tendency to get bored easily, would often throw him off. Even though I was paid well in Germany at my job, I decided to quit and relocate to Vienna because "I've always wanted to go there" as a child. Vienna proved an utter disaster for me, both because I came to hate the city but also because I realized that I hated inauthentic and superficial things. I began to realize that my life needed a massive reevaluation. I wondered why I was obtaining my MA degree in politics in the first place and what exactly I was doing by pursing things I did not want to pursue. Once again, I was flabbergasted by my understanding that everything I knew was very little to what was really out there.

In Berlin, in school, I was surrounded by personally ambitious, yet very hypercritical, individuals who would end up doing whatever to get to where they wanted to go. I would attend high profile meetings with presidents, prime ministers, political ministers of all kinds, and we would shrink in their shadows as they spoke. Everything was so close, and yet so far away, exclusive for them but not for us, although if we worked hard enough, so the saying goes, we would be them. And many of my classmates did work hard enough; they said the right words, and did the right things, and they're now in powerful positions across the globe. But I was disillusioned by this game which sickened me and made me weary of my future. Being what I am, I don't like systems, I don't like status quo, and I don't like maintaining anything in bureaucratic terms. I'm all about exploring the new, the uncertain, and the ideally dangerous. I want to see what makes people tick and what illuminates our lives into something meaningful. Being the "next" president is a continuation. Being the "next" billionaire is a continuation. These people hardly do anything worthy; their ideas are not revolutionary and life-changing. I saw, perhaps eerily, that I was destined to be an authoritive dictator of some sort. Perhaps my Ethiopian professor was right- perhaps I was a Robespierre. And if that's true, then I am obligated, at least externally, to avoid politics for the sake of others. I don't desire to be corrupt. I don't desire to harm anyone. I only desire to make people think for themselves and consider what their motivations are for doing things.

I graduated with my MA in International Relations and Cultural Diplomacy in 2019 and decided not to pursue politics. I instead wandered Europe, looking for odd jobs here and there, while I contemplated my next step. In the meantime, I went back to Romania and reunited with my biological mother (or so I think; given the variety of stories, I am unsure at this point). The meeting with my mother was sour; I noted her manipulative mindset and her victim-oriented personality. Usually, in any other scenario, I would have left the room, but in this case, I had to sit in her house for three hours while she cried and told me how terribly sorry she was about giving me up while my aunts looked at me suspiciously, noting to me later that they never knew I was alive and had never seen me with her. They couldn't believe that I didn't know her, and they couldn't believe that I couldn't speak any Romanian. In the end, my mother scarcely allowed me to speak and any question I asked she seemingly avoided discussing directly, making me feel as if she didn't care about seeing me but rather how she was being perceived around all the other family members. I walked out feeling ashamed that she was my mother. I looked down upon her, and my newly discovered father, who happened to be from Pakistan but was also a German citizen. Nevertheless, I was thrown again into an identity crisis and left wondering what I was exactly and what my true origin legimately was. While all this was happening, I met another girl from Armenia who rejected me without detailing why; I presume because the age difference was significant but also because I was perhaps too intrusive, asking questions that were sharp and made her feel uncomfortable. I questioned her motivations, and it was then that she lost interest in me. I was therefore thrown in a realization that I would probably always be a thorn in peoples' existence, making them feel uncomfortable and uncertain, and for that reason, I will probably always be lonely. Few can stand me, and fewer still have the desire to think as deeply and introspectively as I.

A sudden wave of understanding had passed over me in the following years, as I came to see that people were not obsessed with understanding the philosophical questions as I was. They were not obsessed with authenticity and understanding personal motivations as I was. They were content living their lives centered around themselves and their world, full of passion and their desired purpose. They lived and existed to be, not to question why they were. It is a curse, I suppose. I have always been endowed with, this irritable sickness to ask why. Such a personality is incredibly annoying, incredibly uncomfortable, and incredibly difficult to be in the presence of. It is full of pessimism and cynicism. It is always skeptical and unmotivating for people. To come to terms with these deep questions always means dealing with uncomfortable truths, and for this reason, I am often lonely. Even those who enjoy the occasional chatter and contemplation need a break, for it is often too much. Like a long book, they need to put the volume down and go do something else that doesn't require them to mentally work so intensely. I suppose I understand. For me, as a person, I have always been like this, and I have always increased in sharpness and obsession with questioning everything, perhaps making me a little insane.

I realized very late that everything I do aims to understand the world by confronting it with assertive, ugly lunges. I want to know the why of everything. I cannot help but see connections in the experience of living, from the moans of two people having sex in their apartments to the moans of a woman who lost her child from a war. The smile of my adoptive parents who first laid eyes on me, and the sullen depression they encountered when they had to let me go. The incredible infatuation I held for that girl in college to the incredible pain I felt being confined in a small cold room in Piney Ridge. Somehow, all this is connected. There is a grand theory of things, all wrapped around the experience of a human. I am no scientist; I don't work in a lab. But every time I travel or meet a new person, my mind goes ablaze, taking mental notes and contemplating on them with the greatest scrutiny. I ask why, why people do what they do, for what reason they do it, and what it means in the larger scheme of life. My questions relate to the existential question why do we live and what is our purpose. I feel like if I can answer these questions, I am able to answer an even bigger question how: how we should live and what constitutes a good life. In this way, I recognize my personality fits, almost entirely, to what we would refer to as philosophers. And, regardless of what that word entails and all the grandeur or roll of the eyes it may bring, this is exactly what I am. This is my obsession.

One day, having realized this, I came back to my room wondering why I didn't commit to this pursuit sooner. But then I saw the hundreds of papers with thousands of little words written on them, scrambled on the floor everywhere, containing my thoughts and ideas about everything I could ever dream of. I realized then that all my life I had been philosophizing. I had thought and wrote with incredible diversity about my experience, amongst the contradictions and ironies that made up the person that I was. And, in this, I felt content. I could now die. I had been a writer and a philosopher all my life, and I had now written enough to share to the world all that I was. Everything else was decorative explanations.

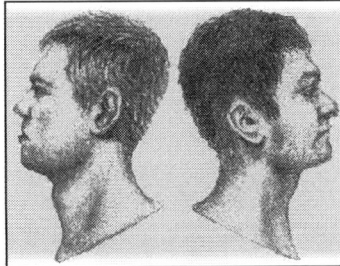

STENDHAL
CLASSICS

Niclas Engelken & Nicolae Burcea

Haren | Germany

stendhalclassics@gmail.com

USt-IdNr.: DE330531881

-

Copyright © 2021, 3rd Edition

STENDHAL **C**LASSICS

All rights reserved.

Printed by Amazon Italia Logistica S.r.l.
Torrazza Piemonte (TO), Italy